Flowers on Tuesday

52 Things I Wish my Father had Taught Me about Marriage & Family

ILYNMW Publishing
Atlanta - Georgia

Dedication:

This book is dedicated to the love of my live – my Bride Debbie!

ILYNMW

YAMBFES

TFSY

Published by: ILYNMW Publishing

www.ILYNMW.com

Copyright 2013   by Paul Beersdorf

v24.0

Our commitment – minimum of 25% of all profits to Charity

Cover Photo: Debbie Beersdorf

Cover Design: Paul Beersdorf

ISBN 978-0-9913244-0-8

Contents

Sections and Chapters

Section One: The Little Things that Matter

Section Two: Listening and the Things we Say

Section Three: How we Spend our Time

Section Four: Spiritual Intimacy

Section Five: Physical Intimacy

Section Six: The Things You Need to do and Remember

Section Seven: How we Spend our Money

Section Eight: Final Thoughts

Bonus Chapter

Acknowledgements:

I have read so many authors and listened to so many preachers in the past years that I cannot distinguish which of these ideas are original and which come from someone else. Certainly there are very few "new" things that I am explaining in these pages, and I freely admit that most of the really good stuff has come from others.

If I can remember whose idea I am using, I will give them credit. It is not my intention to take credit for someone else's work or ideas.

Some of the people I want to recognize are as follows:

Pastor Johnny Hunt – he is an incredible teacher and has been a huge influence in my life and in this book

James Dobson
Dave Ramsey
Tim & Beverly LaHaye
Andy Stanley
Ed Wheat
Gary Smalley
John Trent
Junior Hill
Eric Helms
Rick Stepat
Rick Bellerjeau
Adam Biesecker

And many others!

I also do not want to forget my Bride whom I dedicated this book to. She is my constant companion and best friend. She always believes in me and has encouraged me in all my endeavors. I am a better man because of her.

Finally, I also want all the readers to know that we are committed to donating a minimum of 25% of all the profits to charity.

Preface:

This book is written from the perspective of a Christian husband and the things that he needs to do to make his marriage and family a success. That does not mean that women cannot and will not find this book helpful (as many of the principles are just as easily applied from the wife's perspective), but it has been my experience that most men are in "need" of help when it comes to developing and nurturing the marriage and family relationship.

These principles are things that I have found to be true in my 20+ years of marriage. If I was only smart enough to read and follow my own list on a daily basis I know that I could do an even better job at my marriage. I know there are many more principles, but these are the ones that have been most poignant in my life and it is my prayer that they will help you in your marriage as well.

I have heard it said that the three things that cause the most stress in a marriage are issues related to:

Intimacy
Money
Children

You will find that we discuss each of these subjects in this book.

However, this book is not intended to be an in-depth study on marriage. It is meant to be more of a thought starter and idea generator on how to improve your marriage by incorporating these ideas and suggestions. You will find that I will be pointing you towards other resources to gain deeper knowledge and understanding.

This is not rocket science and we are not going to split the atom or cure cancer. These are just simple ideas and principles learned over 20+ years. I am eternally grateful for all those who have spoken into my life and helped me in these areas.

I hope you enjoy the book and take the opportunity put these principles into action.

The Little Things that Matter

Chapter 1

Flowers on Tuesday

We will start here with something simple in concept but requires forethought and planning. If you do this one thing, I promise you will be amazed at that response you get from your Bride and the sense of pride and accomplishment you will feel yourself.

I honestly don't know if this thought is original with me, or if I read it somewhere and just put it into practice. I would like to take credit for it, but alas I really don't know if I was the one who came up with this idea.

It is very simple: You buy your Bride a bouquet of flowers (preferably roses) and give them to her on Tuesday. What is the significance of Tuesday? Nothing! And that is the point (it could just as easily be any other day of the week, but Tuesday seems to be a day when not much is happening).

The point of giving the flowers on Tuesday is that it is supposed to be a surprise and expression of your love for your Bride. She will not be expecting it and because this is not a special day (e.g. Birthday, Anniversary, or other celebration) she will want to know why you bought the flowers. This is where you tell her, it is just because you love her and want to give here something special.

There are some caveats to this practice (a few of which I have already mentioned):

1. It cannot be her Birthday
2. It cannot be your Anniversary
3. It cannot be a holiday or other special occasion
4. It cannot be something you give her to apologize after a fight or argument
5. It cannot be something you give her because you made a mistake or error
6. It cannot be something you give before you make a big change or announcement

7. It cannot be something you give her just because you want to "get lucky"

This will only work if you give her the flowers – just because!!   Just because you love her.

The funny thing is, she will suspect some of the reasons above the first time you try this (as will the people selling you the flowers.   I cannot tell you how many times someone at the check-out counter will say – "Celebrating an Anniversary" or "Are you in Trouble").   When I explain it is just flowers on Tuesday, and just because I love my Bride, there is the invariable sigh from the female clerks.

Homework: Give it a try.   I usually go to Wal-Mart and get a dozen roses for about $10.   You can just as easily pick flowers from your garden or the side of the road.   Good luck.   I know you will enjoy the response.

Chapter 2

Never let the kids come Between you (Literally and Figuratively)

Debbie and I have four wonderful, beautiful and amazing children. They are:

Hannah – 21
David – 20
Sarah Grace – 12
Jonathan – 10

What a joy and blessing (and to be truthful – challenge) these guys have been. They each have a unique personality and yet they have one thing in common. They are constantly testing us and trying to see if they can drive a wedge between me and my Bride. Now they are not always malicious or thoughtful in this endeavor, it is more a subconscious desire to pit us one against the other.

You see, the kids want and desire our attention (this is a good thing) but only to a point. My first relationship is with my Bride and I constantly need to nurture and develop this relationship. One day the kids will be grown and gone (hopefully) and it will be just me and my Bride alone again.

What Debbie and I have found is that it is best to keep the kids from coming between us. I mean that literally! Whether we are sitting a church, out to eat, or on the couch, Debbie and I ALWAYS sit next to one another. The kids sit on either side of us (usually boys side and girls side).

Now this may seem silly to some of you, but it is subtle and constant reminder that Debbie is my #1 relationship priority. That does not mean that I do not love my children, it just means that there is a pecking order and Debbie is at the top of the list.

Genesis 2:24 - *For this reason a man shall leave his father and his mother, and be joined to his wife; and they shall become one flesh.*

You see, when we married, we became ONE and Debbie is now my best friend and soul mate. She is #1!

The other way that the kids try to come between us is usually with questions and ideas. A simple example is Jonathan coming to me and asking if he can have "a treat". While this may seem innocent and many times it is, we have found that they will try to play us off one another. My usual refrain is "what did Mom say?" This stops them dead in their tracks, because they know if they lie, then they are in even bigger trouble and their reply is usually "she said I had to clean my room first, or mom said No". You see, they are trying to undermine their mother's authority by coming to me and hoping I will simply say "Sure have a treat".

Since we have been doing this parenting thing for 20+ years now, we know most of the tricks.

The other thing we never do is contradict one another in front of the kids. If we have a disagreement then we have a private conversation and gain alignment between ourselves. It is very important that we present a unified front to the kids and that they know without a doubt that I have mom's back and she has my back.

Do you let your kids come between you? Ask yourself why and in what situations.

Homework: Starting today, create a united front and draw closer to your Bride and let the kids know she is the priority relationship.

Chapter 3

Have pet names for each other - Signs, Symbols etc.

This is a simple chapter about closeness. There is no easy way to tell you how to do this. It is something that comes with time and experience.

While I will not share with you the pet names we have for one another (those are private and personal). I will share with you some of the other things that we do that help make our relationship unique and special.

We have our own song. It is the Beatles "I Want To Hold Your Hand". You will see the significance of this later in the book.

One of the things that we have is a little sign that I do from across a room or auditorium and it clearly communicates my love for my Bride. It is a quick hand motion with my finger pointing to my eye and then towards my heart and then at her. It looks like the letter "C" when it is done quickly. It means " I Love You". Her response is to hold up two fingers. This means " I Love You Too".

It may seem simple, sappy and silly, but I will tell you that it is very powerful and quite effective! We have taught this to our children as well. It is very cool to do this and see the look on their face. When my son was playing football he would glance into the stands and I would catch his eye and do the hand motions, he would respond by holding up two fingers and we had an immediate emotional connection. Powerful stuff!

I have done this with Debbie on many, many occasion and it is always very sweet.

Here are a few other things that we do as well.

When I want to send a quick text of encouragement and love I send the following:

ILYNMW!

YAMBFES

TFSY

This reads – I Love You No Matter What! You Are My Best Friend Ever Seen. Thanks For Saying Yes.

The "thanks for saying yes" is thanking Debbie for saying "yes" when I asked her to marry me all those years ago.

Her response is:

ILY2

TFA

TFA = Thanks for asking

That is enough gushy stuff. The point is to have something special and unique for each other

Homework: Find a song that best represents your marriage and make that your song. Buy the song and then play it often!

I have the song "I want to hold your hand" on CD and on my phone. Sometimes, when I am driving down the road, I will put the CD in and turn it up loud and then call Debbie. I hold the phone to the radio and play the song to her. It is a simple way to make a quick connection.

Chapter 4

Do the Things your Spouse does not Like to do

We all have things in life that we do not like to do! The wonderful thing about marriage is that you now have a partner who you can lean on. With trust and understanding you can help each other with those things you do not like doing.

Debbie is a full time mother and home schools our children. I have a full time job and work outside the home. However, that does not excuse me from helping my Bride and trying to make her life easier in the process.

Here are some things that my Bride does not like to do that I do:

1. Grocery Shopping – I know it sounds crazy that a man will do the grocery shopping, but she really hates it and I really do not mind. With four kids in the house, we buy a lot of groceries and it is an ongoing struggle to keep enough food and supplies in the house. Here is the really neat thing. I hate putting up the groceries after they are purchased. So when I get home from the store, Debbie and the kids put up the groceries.
2. Keeping the cars maintained. This means making sure the cars are serviced and maintained so they are in good working order. We tend to drive older cars with lots of miles, so this is critical for Debbie's peace of mind. The last thing she wants is to be broken down on the side of the road.
3. Taxes and everyday bills. This is something that she loathes!! The key to doing this one is that we discuss these items and we both have an understanding of where the money is going.
4. Things I help with around the house:
   a. Laundry – again with 6 of us in the house these is always a ton to do.
   b. Cooking – again with a large household, lots of people to feed all the time.
   c. Cleaning – bathrooms, kitchen etc.

To be clear, these are only examples of things that I do. Your list will most likely be very different from mine. Am I perfect? NO!! Far from it. The key for me is to be intentional, aware and sensitive to her needs.

Finally, you will note that my list does not contain yard work. I hate yard work with a passion! Debbie realizes this and takes this task off my plate – because she likes working in the yard.

The key is helping each other and realizing that as a team, you can accomplish so much more and be more satisfied at the end of the day.

What can you start doing today ? This week? The point is to get started today and help your Bride.

Homework: If you do not already know what your Bride does not like to do, then find out this week what those thing are. Once you find out, create a plan so that you can consistently help her with these things.

Chapter 5

Turn the Coffee on in the Morning

Some of you may be scratching you head on this one. It is very simple. I do not drink coffee, I do not like coffee!!

However, my Bride **LOVES** coffee! She starts her day with 2 big cups each morning and then she is ready to take on the day!

One of the easy ways for me to show my love for my Bride, it to get up before her and start the coffee. Then when she wakes up, she smells the coffee and knows that I love her (or I am at least thinking about her). She sees this as an act of love because she knows I do not drink coffee and the only reason I would do this, is because she is my best friend and I want to do something special for her.

It is a very simple thing to do each day that puts a smile on her face and warms her heart.

It may not be turning on the coffee, but what can you do for your Bride today that will show her your love and commitment in a simple, yet effective way?

If you don't know, don't be afraid to ask her. My guess is that she will have an idea for you.

Homework: find that one special thing that might on the surface appear to be boring and mundane, but will speak volumes to your Bride about your love and commitment to her. Then start doing it!

Chapter 6

Learn to Compromise

Marriage is all about compromise. Unfortunately, for me I did not realize this until a few years into our marriage. The funny thing is that Debbie and I have never had any real arguments about how to raise the kids, where to go to church or other "big things", it was the little things that we fought and complained about.

Looking back now it seems silly, but at the time we has some big battles over the four "T's"

Debbie and I had very different parents and were raised very differently. Therefore when we go married, we had a lot to learn about one another. Our early battles raged around these four T's

What are the four "T's?

- The four T's – toothpaste, toasters, towels, and toilet paper

<u>Toothpaste</u> – Debbie liked to squeeze the toothpaste from the middle, bottom or any other way to get the paste out. I however, squeeze from the bottom so that you can maximize the amount of toothpaste used from each tube. You can imagine how I felt when I saw a tube squeezed from the middle. That was not how it was done! Stupid arguments would follow.

The compromise was very simple – we now each have our own tube of toothpaste.

<u>Toaster</u> – I like to toast bread and bagels for breakfast. I placed the toaster on the counter and left if there, because it was something that I would use all the time. Debbie informed me that appliances were to be put under the counter after use so that the kitchen would be neat and tidy.

We I just thought that was stupid and said so! Why would I put the toaster up, it I was just going to use it again the next day. That was not logical (the same logic that says, why make the bed each day since you are just going to get back in it later that evening).

Debbie explained to me how important it was to her, to have a neat and tidy kitchen and that putting up the toaster after each use is not a huge exercise.

She was right!

The compromise was easy in the end. It was not a battle worth fighting and the toaster now lives under the counter.

<u>Towels</u> – I did not know there was even a way to "handle" a bath towel after it was used. It was not long into our marriage that I was informed that after a towel is used; it should be neatly folded and placed on the towel rack. Wow, what a revelation for me! I had been flinging the used towel over the shower door all my life. To make a long story short, Debbie soon realized that this was not a battle worth fighting and towels never got hung up on the towel bar.

Toilet Paper – this one befuddled me!!! I had no idea that anybody had an opinion about whether the toilet paper should come "over the top" or "from the bottom" when it is placed on the holder. Debbie most definitely had an opinion – over the top! This was an easy compromise for me. I did not care, so it was very easy to make sure when I replaced the toilet paper that it always came over the top.

Now that I know this, when I go to a friend's house and they have a strong opinion about their toilet paper, I always make sure to change it so as to bring a little controversy into their lives. Just Kidding!

These are all fun and silly to talk about, but they are used to point out that there are many simple areas in our lives where we need to compromise and not make everything a battle. Pick and choose your battles carefully. You will find in the long run that it is much better to compromise than fight.

Do you compromise or must you win every battle?

I would encourage you to start learning to compromise today. You will have a much happier and healthier marriage.

Homework: Find an area of conflict in your marriage today and come up with a healthy and viable compromise.

Chapter 7

The "to do" list is not Done Until the mess is Cleaned up

This will be a very short chapter.

Debbie wanted me to build her a set of book shelves. It was a fun project and I took over the garage with all my tools and wood. I completed the book shelves and gave them to her. Unfortunately, I left the mess in the garage for quite a while. This drove her crazy and thus introduced a new principle into my life.

It was not enough to just complete the task, but I needed to clean up afterwards. It was a very simple thing for me to do, and not a lot of extra work on my part. It made her very happy and I like making my Bride happy.

Simple concept: - When you have a "honey do" list, complete the list in a timely fashion and make sure you clean up any mess associated with completing the task.

<u>Homework:</u> Clean up your messes!

Listening and the Things we Say

Chapter 8

50,000 Words

I have heard it many times before that women in general use twice as many words per day as men. It starts out at an early age. If you listen to a little boy, you will find that about half of the sounds that come out of his mouth are just that - sounds (gun shots, lasers, car noises or just funky sounds). A little girl however will almost always use words.

I for one did not believe this until I had children. Then I closely watched my youngest daughter and son and found this to be incredibly true! It really is quite humorous once you know what is going on.

A good example is my teenagers.

When I ask my teenage son how his day at work went, I usually get a mono-symbolic response – "Good" or "OK", or "Fine". And that is the end of the conversation. Now being a man, this level of communication works just fine for me.

However, when I ask my teenage daughter how her day at work went, I get an unending torrent of words starting from the time she left home (not leaving out any detail) until the time she walked in the door. It is a flood of words and I can barely keep up with the story.

So how does the affect us in our marriage?

Well, what I have learned is that I use about 25,000 words per day and my Bride has about 50,000 words she needs to use per day. However, because she is at home with the kids all day, she does not get to use her full allotment of adult conversation, so when I get home she has about 25,000 words for me. On the other hand, I have been gone all day, and have used almost all of my words for the day, so I am "done".

This is where there is real potential for conflict.

I have learned (note this is a learned response for me and not natural – which still frustrates my Bride), to ask how her day has gone, and then take a seat and sit back and listen. I also need to be prepared to offer details of my day with at least one "intricate" story that includes all of the details.

Full discloser here – after 20+ years, I am still not very good at this! I constantly fail and do not listen and respond as I should. However, it is something I want to be good at and something that I will endeavor to improve upon, until the day I die.

Take my advice and learn to become a good listener and a good communicator of you day! Your Bride will appreciate it very much and you will find that it will enhance and improve your relationship.

Homework: Listen, listen, and listen.

Chapter 9

Listen Without Solving

In the previous chapter I spoke about 50,000 words. This chapter is about our response to those words.

I am a solver! I love solving problems, especially other people's problems. I think I am pretty good at it, however I must admit that I am not as good at solving my own problems.

With that said, when Debbie and I first got married, she always seemed to be relating and expressing her problems. This was great, because it gave me an opportunity to solve and accomplish something for my Bride.

Unfortunately, what happened most of the time is that Debbie was not looking for a solution. She just wanted to talk about the problem. To say I found this frustrating and curious would be an understatement. I cannot tell you how many times this would drive me crazy!!

She would tell me, "I don't need you to solve this". My refrain would be something to the effect "then why tell me??" Needless to say, this was not and **is not** the right answer.

Finally it dawned on me that I should be "listening without solving". However, I was not smart enough to know those situations when I should only be listening and those situations when I should be solving.

I came up with what I thought was a logical solution. I would ask her!

So I did.

The next time she had a problem and started to describe it to me, I asked her – "am I listening or am I solving?"

She was taken back a bit, and looked at me like I had three heads. She then said "you should just know"?

We then had a really good dialog around the fact that I was basically a knucklehead and did not know when to listen or when to solve and if she would help me, then we could have much more productive conversations.

When she realized I was not kidding, the light bulb went off above her head and she knew that I needed to ask that question "am I listening or am I solving"?

This really has revolutionized our conversation. Knowing that I don't have to solve a problem takes a real burden off my shoulders and allows me to focus on just listening. Also, when she has a real problem that needs to be solved I can jump right in and give advice and help.

It is a simple concept that has gone a long way to improving our communication and marriage.

Give it a try and see how well it works for you.

Homework: Talk to your Bride this week about listening without solving and what to expect the next time she comes to you with an issue.

These next chapters are the "LEARNING TO" chapters. It is all about learning what to say and making these words an integral part of your vocabulary. These are very powerful words and if you are already using them, then I congratulate you. If you are not using them, I implore you to seek out the opportunity to use them and make them part of who you are! You Bride will surely be grateful.

Chapter 10

Learn to tell your Bride that she is Beautiful

Let me give you some quotes from the Bible – The Song of Solomon:

1:15 – How beautiful you are, my darling, How beautiful you are!

4:1 – How beautiful you are, my darling, How beautiful you are! (Read all of chapter 4 as Solomon describes his Bride)

6:4 – You are as beautiful as Tirzah, my darling, As lovely as Jerusalem, As awesome as an army with banners

You should read Song of Solomon Chapter 7 – another vivid description of the beauty of Solomon's Bride.

In this book Solomon and his Bride talk to one another and love one another.   While we many not immediately understand all of the references and ideas, it is clear that Solomon wants to compliment his Bride and tell her how beautiful she is!

You can never go wrong when you sincerely compliment you Bride and remind her how beautiful she is and that she is the only one for you!

I am a very lucky man! God has blessed me with a Beautiful Bride, be even more so, she is a woman who loves God and her family! Proverbs 31 tells us that "Charm is deceptive and beauty if fleeting; but a woman who fears the Lord is to be praised".   I praise God for my Bride!

I told you in an earlier chapter that Debbie and I have pet names for each other and I would not tell them to you. However, now is the appropriate time to share one of my pet names for Debbie. I call her my "Beautiful Bride". When I send her a text, I send it to my BB (BB = Beautiful Bride). It is a constant reminder to her that I still believe she is the Bride of my youth and amazingly beautiful. It is a constant reminder to me that she is my one true love.

I cannot tell you "how" to tell your Bride that she is beautiful; I can only tell you that you need to do it!

Start today and you will be a better man for it.

Homework: Call, text, e-mail or tell your Bride in person how beautiful she is!

Chapter 11

Learn to say "I love You" Every Day

I have heard it said that a woman's greatest desire is for security. Telling her that you love her each and every day goes a long way towards filling her emotional security bank.

Men are just different creatures. Debbie told me that she loved me on our wedding day and I have been good to go these past 20+ years! I don't need for Debbie to tell me every day or multiple times per day that she loves me. I am just wired very differently from her.

However, I have learned that she wants, needs and desires for me to tell her those three magic words "I Love You". As a matter of fact, if the truth be told, she wants to hear it multiple times each day.

I accomplish this by reminding myself that she is not me and this is a very real need and desire for her. When I send her a text I put – ILYNMW = I Love You No Matter What.

With this little acronym – ILYNMW – not only do I affirm my love for my Bride, I also let her know that it is unconditional. I have been doing this for almost our entire marriage. I profess that I don't get it, but that is not the point. I don't have to get it, I just have to do it.

Look for opportunities to tell your Bride that you love her (and not just when you are being intimate or you just want to be intimate). These are powerful words that need to used multiple times each day.

Here are some ideas:

In the morning – tell your Bride that you love her when you wake up

Before you leave for work – tell your Bride that you love her

Leave her a post-it note on the coffee machine that says – I love you

Call her from your cell phone and just say – "I just wanted to say – I love you" and then hang up

Send her a text and tell her that you love her

Find out where her car is parked and leave a love note in the car for her.

These are not very creative or original ideas but they can be useful and powerful if you try them. Better yet, come up with your own original way to tell your Bride that you love her.

It can be lot of fun and it will only grow and strengthen your marriage.

Homework: See how many times this week you can tell your Bride that you love her. See how many creative ways you can tell her you love her.

Chapter 12

Learn to say "I'm Sorry"

How many times have I hurt my Bride? I hate to admit that it is many more times than I can possibly count. For me it is almost always something mean, cruel or stupid that I say to my Bride. There are other times when I do something stupid, but for the purpose of this chapter I want to focus on things I say. These are the things I will need to say I am sorry for.

Nobody I know would say that I am a very sensitive person. I wear my feeling on my shoulders, and will not shy away from an argument or confrontation. My Bride on the other hand is very sensitive, quiet, thoughtful and hates confrontation and arguments. In other words, there are lots of opportunities for conflict and for me to completely run over her.

When I was younger, I could insult and hurt my Bride and I would not even be aware of the effects that my words or actions were having on her. I was that insensitive!

However, I have learned to say "I'm sorry", because I don't enjoy my relationship with my Bride when there is conflict and I have hurt her. The longer we are married, the easier it has become to say "I'm sorry". I know her better and I know those things that are hurtful and harmful to her. Also, as we grow closer in our relationship, when I hurt her, I am really just hurting myself.

This will not be a profound statement, but I want to state it anyway – Words mean things! Wow, what a revelation right? What we say and how we say it can have a profound impact on the ones we love. Learn to say "I'm sorry" and mean it!

Here is some friendly advice on things **_not_** to say that you will later need to say "I'm Sorry" for:

Any comment about her body that is not positive – keep it to yourself! She does not need to hear it – she is well aware of her shortcoming and only needs to get positive affirmation from you (remember the chapter about telling your Bride she is beautiful)

Any comment that is not positive about her:

> Clothing choices
> Cooking choices
> Decorating choices
> Movie, TV or music choices

I have made foolish, stupid, cruel and mean comments about all of the above! Learn from my mistakes and do not go down these roads. They only lead to pain!

However, if you do go down this road – go ahead and learn the two words for this chapter – "I'm sorry".

Homework: Is there anything you need to say "I'm sorry" for? Don't wait, go ahead and take the time this week to say those magic words.

Chapter 13

Learn to say "I was Wrong"

Learning to say "I was wrong" is different than the previous chapter on saying "I'm sorry".

Not being able to admit you were wrong is all about pride! I always like to look to Proverbs when it comes to the issue of pride:

Proverbs 11:2 – When pride comes, then comes dishonor, But with the humble is wisdom.

Proverbs 16:18 – Pride goes before destruction, And a haughty spirit before stumbling.

Proverbs 29:23 – A man's pride will bring him low, But a humble spirit will obtain honor

Why is it so difficult to admit we are wrong? I know for me, sometimes I just like to "guess" at the answer and then just stick with that answer, even in the face of reality and facts.

What is the answer to pride? The answer is the exact opposite – humility. It is easy to see that from the scripture verses above.

I can honestly say in our marriage that I have had to admit I was wrong much more than Debbie.

With me it really is all about pride. I have learned over time the truth of the following saying:

"I don't know, what I don't know".

Let me put this in context. I can easily say, "I don't know what I don't know about football". In other words, with pride I could pretend that I am an expert at football and argue and fight or I can admit that I still have a lot to learn about football. Now you can substitute any word you want in that statement instead of the word football:

I don't know what I don't know about- Women
I don't know what I don't know about -Relationships
I don't know what I don't know about – The Bible
I don't know what I don't know about - Math
I don't know what I don't know about – History
I don't know what I don't know about – directions
I don't know what I don't know about - plumbing

Admitting you don't know it all is the first step towards humility, understanding and wisdom. And all three of these are key character qualities for a successful marriage.

I came home from work one day in a foul mood and I was itching for a "fight". If we had had a dog, I would have probably kicked it. Instead I just unloaded on my kids. It was both barrels and they were stunned. I stormed off into the bedroom and left Debbie to deal with the aftermath of my destruction. It took me about 10 minutes to cool down and realize I had made a terrible mistake. I had a choice, I could admit I was wrong and say I was sorry and ask for forgiveness or let pride sink its long tentacles into my thinking.

To God be the glory, pride did not win this day. I went back into the living room and gathered all my children and Bride around me and told them how wrong I had been and that my actions were not worthy of the kind of father they deserved. There were many tears, but in the end it was a sweet time of reconciliation and forgiveness.

Homework: swallow your pride this week and admit to your Bride what you are wrong about.

Chapter 14

Learn to say "I Forgive You" – and Mean it!

When you are so close to someone and you know them so well, that can be an incredible blessing. However, because you know your Bride so well, it is also very easy to hurt her. It is easy, because you know the key vulnerable spot in her life and can just poke at it and know it will bother her greatly. She can also do this to you as well.

Have you ever been harmed by your Bride?

I will give you some good biblical guidance on forgiveness at the end of the chapter, but I thought it would be informative to show you what others have to say about forgiveness. Some of these are quite good

Everybody recognizes that forgiveness is powerful.

"There is no love without forgiveness, and there is no forgiveness without love." - Bryant H. McGill

"A happy marriage is the union of two good forgivers." - Robert Quillen

"Forgiveness is me giving up my right to hurt you for hurting me." - Anonymous

"Forgiveness is the giving, and so the receiving, of life." - George MacDonald

"To forgive is to set a prisoner free and discover that the prisoner was you." - Louis B. Smedes

"We are all on a life long journey and the core of its meaning, the terrible demand of its centrality is forgiving and being forgiven." - Martha Kilpatrick

"To forgive is the highest, most beautiful form of love. In return, you will receive untold peace and happiness." - Robert Muller

"Forgiveness is the fragrance the violet sheds on the heel that has crushed it." - Mark Twain

"Always forgive your enemies - nothing annoys them so much." - Oscar Wilde

"The weak can never forgive. Forgiveness is the attribute of the strong." - Mahatma Gandhi

"Forgiveness is a funny thing. It warms the heart and cools the sting." - William Arthur Ward

"Forgiveness does not change the past, but it does enlarge the future." - Paul Boese

"It is easier to forgive an enemy than to forgive a friend." - William Blake

"If you can't forgive and forget, pick one." - Robert Brault

"He who cannot forgive breaks the bridge over which he himself must pass." - George Herbert

"Without forgiveness life is governed by... an endless cycle of resentment and retaliation." - Roberto Assagioli

"Forgive all who have offended you, not for them, but for yourself." - Harriet Nelson

"Life is an adventure in forgiveness." - Norman Cousins

"Forgiveness is the key to action and freedom." - Hannah Arendt

"Forgiveness is a virtue of the brave." - Indira Gandhi

"As long as you don't forgive, who and whatever it is will occupy a rent-free space in your mind." - Isabelle Holland

"Anger makes you smaller, while forgiveness forces you to grow beyond what you were." - Cherie Carter-Scott

"Forgiveness is like faith. You have to keep reviving it." - Mason Cooley

"Only the brave know how to forgive. ... A coward never forgave; it is not in his nature." - Laurence Sterne

Debbie and I could not have survived these 20+ years of marriage without forgiveness. It is just not possible. We see so many couples who are bitter and angry and never learn to forgive. They truly are the ones who are trapped by their un-forgiveness.

For me, the bible is the best source for guidance on forgiveness. The central theme of the Bible is Christ dying on the cross for our sins and all we have to do is ask forgiveness from our sins and God will forgive us because of what Christ did for us on the cross.

If you have not forgiven your Bride for something, then consider these verses and decide if you can still not forgive.

Should we forgive or not?

Matthew 6:14-15 – [14] For if you forgive others for their transgressions, your heavenly Father will also forgive you. [15] But if you do not forgive others, then your Father will not forgive your transgressions.

Ephesians 4:32 – [32] Be kind to one another, tender-hearted, forgiving each other, just as God in Christ also has forgiven you.

Colossians 3:13 – bearing with one another, and forgiving each other, whoever has a complaint against anyone; just as the Lord forgave you, so also should you.

How many times should we forgive?

Matthew 18:21-22 - [21] Then Peter came and said to Him, "Lord, how often shall my brother sin against me and I forgive him? Up to seven times?" [22] Jesus *said to him, "I do not say to you, up to seven times, but up to seventy times seven.

Finally – How true Love and Forgiveness go hand in hand

1 Corinthians 13-4:5 -[4] Love is patient, love is kind and is not jealous; love does not brag and is not arrogant, [5] does not act unbecomingly; it does not seek its own, is not provoked, does not take into account a wrong suffered,

Love keeps no record of wrongs.

Homework: If you need to forgive your Bride, do not wait, seek her out and forgive her.

Chapter 15

Learn to make "Thank You" a Consistent part of your Vocabulary

Now you would think this would be the easiest thing to do amongst all of the "learn to's". However, I have found the more often than not, I take for granted all the little things my Bride does each and every day.

Most weeks, I have "magic drawers". What are magic drawers? Well, I go to my dresser and I open up the sock drawer, and there are clean socks. I open the underwear drawer and there is clean underwear. Day in and day out, I never seem to run out of clean cloths. And yet….. do I thank my Bride?

The house is clean and uncluttered and the children are obedient and well mannered. And yet ……… do I thank my Bride?

There is good food to eat and a clean kitchen, and yet………… do I thank my Bride?

She is thrifty and thoughtful and constantly looking for ways to help others and make their day better, and yet……………do I thank my Bride?

She meets my physical and emotional needs, and yet………..do I thank my Bride?

She is my constant companion in sickness and in health, and yet ………..do I thank my Bride?

Learn to say thank you to your Bride, for there are many, many things each day to be thankful for!

Homework: My challenge for you today is to look for at least one thing that you can thank your Bride for today. Even the most jaded person can find one thing to be thankful for.

Chapter 16

Praise in Public and Criticize in Private

Debbie and I can always tell when there is obvious strife in a marriage. We can be in Sunday School, a party, at work or wherever, and we will hear someone running down their spouse with criticism. When we are together and we hear this, we give each other a knowing look and sigh with grief knowing that one spouse is tearing down the other in public.

You should never, ever publicly offer criticism of you Bride to others. That is not to say that we should never criticize one another. However, doing so publicly is neither wise nor appropriate. If you have something critical to say to your Bride, then you should look for an opportunity to do so privately. There is nothing to be gained by criticizing in public.

On the other hand, you should take every opportunity to offer praise for you Bride in public (whether she is there or not). You should constantly be looking for opportunities to tell others of the key virtues of your Bride and how wonderful she really is. It is even better if she is with you and she can see and hear you praising her before others. This is especially true in front of close friends and family members.

In the Book of James, he tells us that the tongue cannot be tamed by any man (James 3:8), therefore we should constantly be on guard as to what we say and how we say it.

I remember it this way – PRAISE IN PUBLIC, CRITICIZE IN PRIVATE. A good rule to follow.

<u>Homework:</u> This week look for a way to praise your Bride in public (even if it is only in front of the kids or family)

Chapter 17

Defend your Spouse against Family Members and Friends when Necessary

It has often been said that you can pick your nose, you can pick your friends, but you cannot pick your family. That is very true. We all have families that we were born into (each of us with a crazy Uncle Joe) and when we get married we gain a whole new set of family and all the issues that go along with that.

Genesis 2:24 – For this reason a man shall leave his father and his mother, and be joined to his wife; and they shall become one flesh.

We see so many couples who do not think of themselves as "one". Even worse, there a many parents and family members who still think their Daughter/Niece/Grand Daughter is still fair game for criticism and complaining. This should not be so. Your Bride should not have to stand alone against her family and friends to defend herself.

You are now ONE with your Bride and you should take every opportunity to love and protect her – especially when the attacks come from family and friends. Present a united front and do not let them think that you are party to their barbs and arrows. Instead, be the shield and ward off those angry words.

They have to know that you cannot and will not be taking their side. They have to know that you are committed to your Bride and you will defend her to the bitter end.

Now to be clear, this does not cover every situation. There could be a time when you and your family need to confront your Bride (for example - in a case of obvious addiction/behavior where she could harm herself or others).

However, this is the exception to the criticism and the pain that is usually heaped on by family members and friends (they are especially fond of bringing up the past and all of our short comings)! Praise be to God that **HE** does not do that to us.

To that end, be a defender and always look to protect your Bride.

<u>Homework:</u> Defend you Bride at all times!

How we Spend our Time

Chapter 18

Make Family Vacations Together a Priority

In our family, vacations are an investment! They are an investment in time, they are an investment in memories, and they are an investment in family.

We learned early on (from many of the books and seminars we had attended), that having dedicated time away as a family is a must to refresh and renew relationships. We have to pull away from the world and all of the demands on our time and just focus on each other.

When I was a young husband and father, I remember reading in one of the parenting books about the truths behind successful families. Two of the specific activities these families did were camping and boating. Families mentioned these two activities as the most productive and helpful, because everyone was involved!

I did not grow up camping and I did not grow up boating! But we have done each many many times and believe me; you will create memories (both good and bad). ☺

We do not own a boat, but there is a lake nearby and we rent a boat and go tubing and skiing. We have had some incredible fun and getting caught in a thunderstorm on the lake is definitely a memory. This past summer we decided to go white water rafting. Now my oldest son and I have done this a dozen or so times from our days in Boy Scouts, but we have never been rafting as a whole family together.

Since I was the "expert", we decided to go without a guide and just have our family together in one raft (the level of rapids on this river allowed us to choose this option – though most people do not). We got stuck on rocks, almost flipped the boat a couple of times and had to rescue my youngest son when he fell out. In other words it was a perfect family trip! No cell phones, no distractions, it was only us against the river. It was four hours of terror and bliss! Wow did we create memories!!!

We go to the beach each summer for either one or two weeks. We do not own a condo or house at the beach, we just rent. We have been doing this our entire married life. It is now part of our family DNA. We have been going to the same beach for 20+ years, and we have so many wonderful and incredible memories.

BTW - You do not have to take an expensive vacation. You can stay close to home. One of my favorite memories is the vacation we took as a family. We were going to the mountains (without reservations – my father's modus operandi) and when we go there, everything was booked and sold out. We ended up sleeping in the car (7 of us) and then driving to a city not far from our home and staying in a hotel all week. We went to the movies every night and ate pizza and swam in the pool (I remember watching Star Wars – yes the original).
I know that was not my dad's original plan, but it worked out great.

Do you take vacations?   Are they a priority?

I know too many people who say they are too busy or it is too expensive. I can only say, you will never get that time back and if you do not take the vacation, the time will pass, your kids will be grown and gone and you will have missed the opportunity to create life long memories and develop deeper and more meaningful relationships.

Take the time right now to book a vacation. And when you are on that vacation, leave the job at home! When I go on vacation I do not take my work cell phone or personal cell phone or computer! They are all put into a plastic bag and left at home! I go to Wal-mart and buy a disposable phone so I can stay in touch with my Bride and kids as I run around town on vacation.

Things I don't do on vacation:

I do not check e-mail – ever!

I do not check voicemail – ever!

I do not call and check in at the office –ever!

Since I don't have my cell phone, nobody from work is calling me (remember the phone is in a plastic bag at my house)

How do I do this? I give myself permission! If you were to call my cell phone, my voicemail would say "Hi, sorry I missed your call, but I am on vacation and will return on such and such date, if this is urgent please contact – Person XYX, otherwise I will return your call when I get back from vacation). My e-mail has an auto reply that says the same thing. I have now given myself permission to check out.

For me, I don't know another way to focus. I cannot have part of my mind on work and part of my mind on vacation. It just does not work for me.

My family clearly understands that they are my focus and priority on vacation and it is a clear signal to them of my love and devotion. I am also helping set the tone and example for my children, so they will do the same thing when they are adults.

We all only have 24 hours each day and 365 days each year. If you have not made vacations a priority before, do it this year. I promise you will be blessed.

Homework: plan a vacation for this year. Even if it is a "staycation"

Chapter 19

Have a Date time each Week and Regular Weekends away

I have to give full credit to my pastor (Dr. Johnny Hunt) for these ideas. I have heard him preach and teach about having a regular date night, getting away once a quarter for a long weekend, and a yearly trip.

While we have not been able to take a yearly trip away, we have been able to have a regular date night (usually Friday night) and we have gotten away for quite a few long weekends and retreats.

I usually make a formal request and ask my Bride out for a date! It is fun and silly, but it just reminds us of when we were younger and anticipated the date and the time together. Many times our date nights are not fancy at all! We go to our local Mexican restaurant (where they now know us by name and we don't even have to use a menu any more) and then we either to the thrift store or Wal-Mart. Exciting right!

My Bride LOVES shopping at the thrift store, and I can usually find a good book to read after I have spent about 5 minutes shopping.

The point is to have focused time away from the kids and the rest of the world. Many times we break out our calendars and discuss upcoming events and activities or just talk without distractions (a true luxury). It is just a few hours, but it is a good investment in time

With four kids, getting away for a long weekend requires some planning and fore thought. We just got back from a long weekend in Ashville North Carolina. We visited the Biltmore House for Christmas and it was a great trip! My Bride loved that fact that I would take her to a big house and just walk around for several hours looking at the decorations. For me, it was about investing time with my Bride and doing something special for her.

In the next couple of months we are going to attend a couples retreat at the WinShape resort (which was founded by Chick-fil-a). This is a more purposeful time for us to intentionally focus on making our marriage stronger and growing closer together. We need to continually be "re-filling" our relationship cup so that it will always be full and never grow old.

They say that building a successful business is all about proper allocation of resources. The same is true with a marriage. We have to allocate, time and money and create a plan to succeed. You cannot just stumble through your marriage. You must be intentional about how you will spend your time, how you will spend your money, and building a better marriage.

I have my own saying: "Have a plan and work your plan"

An old saying is: "If you fail to plan, then plan to fail".

I have found both of these to be true.

Homework: If you do not have a regular date night, then start this week (it might be helpful if you give her flowers on Tuesday). Plan a weekend away. You can stay at Motel 6, and go see a couple of movies or go camping and hiking. It does not have to be expensive, you just need to plan something and do it. If you live in the southeast, you can go to: http://www.winshaperetreat.org/ and they always have some good things planned.

Chapter 20

Celebrate all of the "Events" of Life Together.

Let's start with a definition of "events". What do I mean by events? The things listed below are "events":

Marriages
Births
Funerals
Birthdays
Retirement

Some of these things are once in a life time and some are annual. But the main thing is being present with your Bride and making it a priority.

We have been to a lot of weddings lately and not one of them was for someone we were related to. My Bride loves going to weddings and to be honest I barely tolerate going to weddings. But I know that this is very important to her and she loves to hold my hand and look at our rings as the couples say their vows together. I love being with her and doing something that is important to her. She knows that I really don't care for weddings, but she also knows that my love for her supersedes my selfish nature in this area.

I have observed that many men skip going to weddings. I see lots of our friends wife's but not the husbands. I used to be one of those guys.

Then I realized that I was missing an important opportunity to show my love to my Bride and that the time could not be redeemed once it had passed. So I go to weddings now. We laugh, we dance, we eat, and we remember the day when we said our vows. I still do not completely enjoy going to weddings, but I sure do love spending time with my Bride

There are many of these types of events in life where we many not want to attend or feel like attending. My advice to you, go anyway!

Homework: Go ahead and make up your mind that you are going to attend these events and then tell you Bride (she will help hold you accountable)

Chapter 21

Beware of Time Killers

Let me say up front that I know this will be a tough chapter for you to read, and some of you will be upset when you finish reading. I am ok with that! I really want you to do a gut check and determine how you are using your time.

Let's agree up front that we are all busy people! There are only 24 hours in a day and we all have to be very circumspect about how we spend our time. I have found that the following can be time killers in my life if I am not careful (and believe me I have not always been careful).

The list below is not comprehensive, but it is the list that seems to resonate with most people. You can add your own items to the list.

     i.   Job
    ii.   Cell Phone
    iii.   TV
    iv.   Surfing the Web
    v.   Hobbies

Job

We all have to work at our jobs and make a living. Sometimes we have seasons of work when we have to put in more hours than others. For me January through May are unusually busy! I work more nights and some weekends – but it is a season for me and not all year long. If I am not careful, I can spend 16 hours a day pursuing my "career" and "opportunities". For me, the only way I know how to combat this is to be intentional in the day and week about how I spend my time.

I purposefully allocate time for my family on my calendar. Sometimes it is only an hour here or there, but the key is spending time with them. It is not about "quality time" it is about "quantity time". I try to get in as much quantity as possible, because you never know when it will become quality! I cannot tell you how many times I would be riding down the road with my Bride or kids and we would start an awesome discussion or conversation. You can never predict when you will have the quality.

Cell Phones

Most everybody has a cell phone and the majority of people today have a "smart phone". I am very passionate about this subject! I hear people tell me all the time they wish they could control their cell phone time better. They just do not know what to do. I tell them about a magic button that is on each and every cell phone. Do you know what the magic button is??

It is called the OFF button! If you turn your cell phone off, then I guarantee that you will not be bothered by text messages, e-mail messages or phone calls. It works 100% of the time.

I can just hear some of your right now. "Paul – you just do not understand, I have to be in constant contact 24 hours per day –my job requires it".

I agree that there is a small group of people who are truly on call 24/7 and their job requires them to be on call (I think of friends of mine who are doctors, dentists, and military). However, the vast majority of people I know do not need to be on call 24/7.

There is nothing ruder than to be in a conversation with your Bride and to take a call, check a text or email. When you are with her, be with her!

When we go out on dates, I do not even take my phone! You already read earlier what I do with my phone on vacation.

I have just learned that having my phone with me is like having my job with me all the time. So I am very intentional about how I use my phone and when I use my phone.

I know many of you will disagree with me, but my challenge for you is to please learn to be intentional about how and when you use your phone, and show your family that they are more important than a call, text or e-mail.

TV

TV time can be fun when you spend it with family and friends. I will keep this short. What percent of your time do you spend watching things by yourself? What percent of your time do spend watching things with your Bride?

If you enjoy watching sports and she does not enjoy it that much, tell her stories about the players and their lives. You Bride is looking for ways to connect with the players, and understanding their life and stories will help her become more interested.

My Bride loves HGTV! Guess what I watch with my Bride? HGTV. Not every show and not all the time, but there are plenty of shows that we watch together, because this is something that she enjoys and I just love spending time with her.

Make your TV time more productive by spending it with others!

Surfing the WEB

If I am not careful I can spend hours and hours on the WEB! Not only do I have to be careful about the time, I also have to be careful about what I look at on the internet.

Guard your eyes, guard your mind, and guard your heart.

How are you spending your time? What website are you going to? How much time are you spending on the internet?

The internet is an awesome tool! It can be very powerful and useful. It can also bring you down in a heartbeat!

Be careful, beware, and be on guard. All the time

Hobbies

We all need hobbies and time to pursue things we enjoy. Here are some of the things I really enjoy:

Running, Swimming, Biking, Hiking, Camping, Woodworking

There is nothing wrong with any of these hobbies – unless they begin to take over my life and time.

There was a point when I was going to the gym twice a day to work out. While I felt good about myself, it had a negative impact on my Bride and family.

Debbie had to pull me aside and call me out for the amount of time I was spending working out. She loved the fact that I was taking care of myself; she just did not appreciate how much time I was spending and when I was working out.

She was right! I was oblivious to the fact because I thought I was doing something "good".

So what did I do? Well most of the time when I work out now, I take someone with me (one of the kids or Debbie) that way we can spend time together. I also try to schedule my workouts so they do not conflict with family time (especially dinner time).

I still fail sometimes, but I am now aware and try to be very intentional about how and when I exercise.

What is your hobby? Is it something you do alone? Can you include your Bride or kids in your hobby? If so, do you include them? If not, think about why you do not include them and consider whether or not that is a good use of your time.

When I run outside (and not at the gym), most of my running is by myself (because my pace is different from the others, and most of them do not enjoy running outside). However, there are times when my youngest daughter wants to go for a run and I intentionally run at her pace and enjoy the time together.

The whole point of this chapter is to be intentional and thoughtful about how you spend your time. There are many time killers in our life. The first step to being intentional is to gain control of your time and calendar.

You should control your hobbies and not let them control you.

I know I have been somewhat provocative in this chapter, but I want to jolt some of you into thinking about how you spend your time.

I hope you stick with me through the rest of the book.

Homework: Review the time killers in your life and look for ways to adjust your schedule to be more intentional with your time.

Chapter 22

Making Her a Priority

So we just talked about time killers! If you are now committed to being intentional about how you spend your time, now I challenge you to take some of that time to make your Bride a priority.

What do I mean? Isn't she already a priority?

Here is a simple question. If you had to choose between spending time with your Bride or time with your children – which would you choose?

You see, I have already know the answer to this question. I would always choose my Bride!

> *Genesis 2:24 – For this reason a man shall leave his father and his mother, and be joined to his wife; and they shall become one flesh.*

You see, I love my children desperately. But Debbie is the love of my life! I do love her more than I love my children. I have been with her longer than I have been with any of my kids, I have experienced more with her than any of my kids, and most importantly – one day the kids will be grown and gone and it will just be the two of us again (just like it was at the beginning of our marriage).

It's not like I neglect my children or family, it's just that Debbie is and always will be a higher priority than all of them!

I prove to her that she is a priority by doing the following:

- Sending time with her!
- Spending money on her!
- Doing things for her!

Is your Bride a priority in your life? If you were to ask her, would she agree with you? If you were to ask your kids would they agree with you?

You can always tell where your priorities are by looking at the following:

- You bank/checking account
- Your credit card bills
- Your calendar

Where does your Bride rank in these three areas? Are you being intentional?

Let me give you an example that I think ties all of this together.

Debbie LOVES and I mean LOVES musicals and Broadway shows. We live in Atlanta and are lucky enough to have a few good places to actually see these types of shows. Do I like them? I tolerate them. However, because my Bride loves them, I have made this a priority.

This is what I do:

1. I purchase seasons tickets (usually 6-8 shows). This is no small purchase! I am making an investment in my Bride
2. I put all the dates on my calendar and block that time out (usually Saturday evenings)
3. I line up baby sitters to watch the kids
4. I get dress up (this is probably my biggest sacrifice – I prefer shorts and t-shirts)
5. I take her out to eat

I have now been intentional and have a specific date night set up for 6-8 Saturdays for the year. I have invested money and also time on my calendar. Most importantly, I am doing something that she really enjoys. I love spending time with her, so it will always be enjoyable.

Homework: – find something that you can do that will involve some investment of your time and treasure to show your Bride that she is a priority in your life.

You just might enjoy the response you get from her!!

Spiritual Intimacy

Chapter 23

Give of your Time, Talents and Treasures to God's Kingdom Together

It is one thing to just go to through the motions of attending church and quite another to be committed to furthering God's Kingdom.

I heard a really good story about the difference between attendance and commitment:

A Chicken and a Pig lived on a farm. The farmer was very good to them and they both wanted to do something good for him.

One day the chicken approached the pig and said, "I have a great idea for something we can do for the farmer! Would you like to help?"

The pig, quite intrigued by this, said, "of course! What is it that you propose?"

The chicken knew how much the farmer enjoyed a good healthy breakfast. He also knew how little time the farmer had to make a good breakfast. "I think the farmer would be very happy if we made him breakfast."

The pig thought about this. While not as close to the farmer, he too knew of the farmer's love for a good breakfast. "I'd be happy to help you make breakfast for the farmer! What do you suggest we make?"

The chicken, understanding that he had little else to offer suggested, "I could provide some eggs."

The pig knew the farmer might want more, "That's a fine start. What else should we make?"

The chicken looked around...scratched his head...then said, "ham? The farmer loves ham and eggs!"

The pig, very mindful of what this implied, said, "that's fine, but while you're making a contribution I'm making a real commitment!"

Now, I am certainly not advocating that you kill yourself, but I am saying that the true commitment comes with a price. Are you the chicken or the pig when it comes to your time, talents or treasures?

For us that price is tangible in Time, Talents and Treasure. For this to work everybody in the family must be on board and you as the father must lead!

<u>Time</u> – time at church in worship and praise, time with our kids in choir and AWANAs, time in Sunday School, time on mission trips, time at conferences and retreats, time in prayer. Time is probably the most precious commodity we have today. Look at your calendar and you will see where your commitment lies.

<u>Talents</u> – teaching Sunday School, singing, play musical instruments, dancing (yes you can praise God in the dance as well), teaching others, using skills (plumber, lawyer, carpenter, accountant etc.). There are many ways you can use the talents that God has blessed you with.

<u>Treasure</u> – supporting your local church, supporting other local charitable organizations that are reaching others for God, supporting local, national and international missionaries, supporting others to go on short-term mission trips.

I know of one really good way to combat my own greedy and selfish nature – and that is to be generous! I have always told my Bride and children that it is such a blessing to be an answer to a prayer! It blesses you, blesses the other person and God receives the honor and glory! It also constantly reminds me of Gods work and presence in our life.

Let me relate a story within a story.

At our church we have quite a few people who go on short-term missions trips. They are responsible for raising 100% of their support. They typically do this by sending out letters to friends and family and asking for a financial contribution. One of my very favorite Sunday School teachers shared how he had received many of the letters, but did not always make a contribution.

However, one day he and his Bride committed to making a contribution to each and every letter they received. They had no idea that the next week they would receive 15 letters! They made a contribution to each and it was such a blessing to those they supported. When they started to get the follow up notes that people would send after the trip, they could see a direct correlation between their contribution and Gods work on the mission field (both with the people who served and those that were served).

We thought this was a great idea, so we committed to doing the same thing. And this leads to my story within this story.

Normally when we receive a support letter from someone, we will sit right down and send them a check that day. However, one time I had misplaced a letter from a young lady named Macy. It was lost on my desk somewhere. It was several weeks later that I found the letter. It was very sweet and she was excited about her first trip and really felt God calling her to go on this trip. She had a total amount of money to raise (I think it was around $1,500) and she just asked for any level of contribution and prayer. So we mailed her a very specific amount of support and forget about the letter.

A few days later her mother called my Bride and was in tears (of joy we later found out). You see, that afternoon she had picked up Macy at school and Macy was very sad and upset. The mother asked why and Macy said – "Well tonight is our commitment night for the missions trip and I have to have $XXX raised or I cannot go on this trip. I really feel that God has called me to go on this trip, but I have not received any money yet. What am I to do?

Her mother knew exactly what to do! She pulled the car over and they prayed right there on the side of the road. They thanked God for his many blessings and asked that HIS will be done. The mom then said, let's go home and check the mailbox.

You guessed it. There was our letter and the amount of money was exactly what she need at exactly the right time.

If we had not "lost" the letter, then the check would have gotten to her several weeks earlier, but you see, God's timing is so much better than ours! Not only did he increase her faith, he increased the mom's faith, or faith and now hopefully yours! She raised the rest of her money and was able to attend the mission trip!

Being able to contribute our treasures (which come from God to begin with) to promote God's kingdom really is a blessing.

Homework:

Look at your calendar –where can you spend more time helping God's Kingdom

Consider your talents – what skills has God blessed you with that you can use for His glory

Look at your money – where can you invest today to bring God's word to others?

Chapter 24

Routine of Prayer, Praise and Worship Together

It is early Sunday morning as I write this chapter. The house is quiet and I have already been up to do my devotion and prayers. It is a great way to start the day and it sets the tone for my attitude and actions for the rest of the day.

As a family we spend a lot of time together at our church –we attend a fairly large church (about 6,000 – 8.000 each Sunday).

Sunday – Praise and Worship
Monday – none
Tuesday – Timothy Ministry – (this is a home school co-op where parents come together to teach)
Wednesday – mid-week praise, prayer, worship, and various activities
Thursday – Upward sports (when we are in that season)
Friday – only when there are special events
Saturday – only when there are special events

This is our routine as a family. We also pray and do bible studies together and attend various conferences and concerts as well.

In the morning, Debbie will do devotion with the kids and then have a time of prayer (I am usually at work). In the evenings I will pray with the kids.

The one thing that I should do more often and I don't is prayer time with my Bride! I pray alone, I pray with the kids but I don't get enough prayer time with my Bride. It is something that is very special and needs to be part of our regular routine.

I have no excuse and I make not excuse! I am committing to all of you that I will make this part of my routine. Will you join me and committing to pray with your Bride?

Homework: Find a church where you and your family can "plug in" and invest your time, talents and treasures. You have to lead your family and make prayer, praise and worship a priority.

Chapter 25

Pray for Your Bride

I know this may seem obvious to many of you, but I want to be overt and call it out. You need to pray for your Bride!

In full disclosure, I have not always done this very well. It was not until I got a prayer journal and specifically listed out each and every person and situation I need to pray about.

Guess who the first person on my prayer list is? Did you guess Debbie? If you did, then you get bonus points! Debbie is at the very top of my list. I pray for her first, I pray for her the most and I pray for her the deepest. It is my intimate time with God that I lift up my Bride. I know her wants, needs and desires and even if I don't, God does.

How often? You should be praying for your Bride?

Every day!

1 Thessalonians 5:17 – pray without ceasing

I find myself most days praying for her multiple times per day. Sometimes she just comes to my mind and I lift her up in prayer. Prayer can and does change lives. It is powerful and it keeps us grounded in acknowledging God in all things.

Colossians chapter one verses 9-14 give a great example of how to pray for others.

[9] For this reason also, since the day we heard of it, we have not ceased to pray for you and to ask that you may be filled with the knowledge of His will in all spiritual wisdom and understanding, [10] so that you will walk in a manner worthy of the Lord, to please Him in all respects, bearing fruit in every good work and increasing in the knowledge of God; [11] strengthened with all power, according to His glorious might, for the attaining of all steadfastness and

patience; joyously [12] *giving thanks to the Father, who has qualified us to share in the inheritance of the saints in Light.* [13] *For He rescued us from the domain of darkness, and transferred us to the kingdom of His beloved Son,* [14] *in whom we have redemption, the forgiveness of sins.*

Lift your Bride up in prayer, early and often. If you just love your IPhone or Android phone, then consider downloading one of the different prayer APPS that are available. These can prove very helpful as reminders to pray for your Bride throughout the day and week.

Finally, here are some of the on-going things I pray for my Bride:

Wisdom
Discernment
Keep her close and clean
Blessing on her life
Hedge of protection

There are many other very specific things each day and week that I am lifting up in prayer, but the few things above cover a multitude of situations in her day to day living.

Homework: Will you commit to praying for your Bride? If so, go and buy a notebook to record your prayers and thoughts. Also ask your Bride if there are any specific things she would like you to pray for in her life.

Physical Intimacy

Chapter 26

Remember the Bride of your Youth

*Proverbs 5:18 - Let your fountain be blessed, And rejoice in the wife (**Bride**) of your youth.*

I substitute the word Bride for wife and I have this verse imprinted on my heart and mind! How easy is it for us to forget why we were attracted to our Bride and why we pursued them and wanted them to be our one and only love.

We stood before our family and friends and made a commitment "for better or worse", in "sickness and in health". Were these just words or were these commitments with you heart and mind.

Debbie and I have been married for 20+ years now and I can honestly say I love her more today than the day we were married. Why? Because we have been through so much together and we have grown closer through the good times and the bad times.

How many men get to my age and think about trading in their 50 year old Bride for a newer 25 year old model? They think the grass will be greener on the other side and somehow it will make them feel like they are not a 50 year old man.

I want to let you in on little secret. There will always be someone younger, whose body is firm and hair is not colored. This will never change! Never! So now that you know the secret, you can just take it out of your consideration set. You cannot be fooled or tricked. You know the secret.

What do you need to do?

Here is my list of "Do not's"

- Don't put yourself in situations where you are spending a lot of time with younger women (either married or not).
- Don't focus on the negative aspects of your Bride – focus on her strengths
- Don't let your guard down – ever! You will have to be on guard the rest of your life. It only takes a minute to make a stupid mistake.
- Don't let your mind wander into fantasy land. It is just that – a fantasy!
- Don't let your eyes wander (see next chapter)
- Don't let your lips wander – the words– you know when you are flirting, so just stop it before it goes too far.
- Don't let your lips wander – the kiss– no it is not just an innocent kiss. Kissing is very intimate and should be reserved for your Bride alone (some consider kissing more intimate than intercourse)
- Don't let your hands wander – keep them to yourself and your bride. Don't offer that back rub to your team mate who is just "so tense"
- Don't become an emotional "crutch" for another woman. She does not need your shoulder to lean on! This is a path that will lead to destruction.
- Don't forget the impact your actions will have on your Bride but also on your children and family. Too many men do not consider the cost!

If you feel like there is not enough romance or love in your marriage, don't look any farther than the mirror! It is your responsibility to drive the romance and love in your marriage.

I know what my weaknesses are and I must constantly keep up my guard! **"But for the Grace of God go I"**

Am I perfect? No! Have I failed – you bettcha! When I fail it is an exercise in asking forgiveness and rebuilding the relationship. While I will not recount my sins and failures – I will only say that I have never had a physical affair but there are plenty of other ways to fail and not honor the Bride of my youth. Just because you don't have a physical relationship with another woman does not mean you are innocent of either "mental adultery or visual adultery".

Be on guard – always!   Put on the full armor of God

Ephesians 6:10-17

The Armor of God

[10] *Finally, be strong in the Lord and in the strength of His might.* [11] *Put on the full armor of God, so that you will be able to stand firm against the schemes of the devil.* [12] *For our struggle is not against flesh and blood, but against the rulers, against the powers, against the world forces of this darkness, against the spiritual forces of wickedness in the heavenly places.* [13] *Therefore, take up the full armor of God, so that you will be able to resist in the evil day, and having done everything, to stand firm.* [14] *Stand firm therefore, HAVING GIRDED YOUR LOINS WITH TRUTH, and HAVING PUT ON THE BREASTPLATE OF RIGHTEOUSNESS,* [15] *and having shod YOUR FEET WITH THE PREPARATION OF THE GOSPEL OF PEACE;* [16]*in addition to all, taking up the shield of faith with which you will be able to extinguish all the flaming arrows of the evil one.* [17] *And take THE HELMET OF SALVATION, and the sword of the Spirit, which is the word of God.*

If need be, - flee!

2 Timothy 2:22

Now flee from youthful lusts and pursue righteousness, faith, love and peace, with those who call on the Lord from a pure heart.

Here is an example of what to do.

Genesis 39 1-12

Now Joseph had been taken down to Egypt; and Potiphar, an Egyptian officer of Pharaoh, the captain of the bodyguard, bought him from the Ishmaelites, who had taken him down there. [2] *The LORD was with Joseph, so he became a successful man. And he was in the house of his master, the Egyptian.* [3] *Now his master saw that the LORD was with him and how the LORD caused all that he did to prosper in his hand.* [4] *So Joseph found favor in his sight and became his personal servant; and he made him overseer over his house, and all that he owned he put in his charge.* [5] *It came about that from the time he made him overseer in his house and over all that he owned, the LORD blessed the Egyptian's house on account of Joseph; thus the LORD'S blessing was upon all that he owned, in the house and in the field.* [6] *So he left everything he owned in Joseph's charge; and with him there he did not concern himself with anything except the food which he ate.*

Now Joseph was handsome in form and appearance. [7] It came about after these events that his master's wife looked with desire at Joseph, and she said, "Lie with me." [8] But he refused and said to his master's wife, "Behold, with me here, my master does not concern himself with anything in the house, and he has put all that he owns in my charge. [9] There is no one greater in this house than I, and he has withheld nothing from me except you, because you are his wife. How then could I do this great evil and sin against God?" [10] As she spoke to Joseph day after day, he did not listen to her to lie beside her or be with her. [11] Now it happened one day that he went into the house to do his work, and none of the men of the household was there inside. [12] She caught him by his garment, saying, "Lie with me!" And he left his garment in her hand and fled, and went outside.

What else can I say? Be the man that your Bride, children and family can be proud of. Choose to be a positive example in the crazy world where men are leaving their Brides in record numbers. Choose to be a positive statistic.

Homework: work this week on putting on the full amour of God and keeping it on!

Chapter 27

Guard your Eye Gates

As men we are visual creatures. We notice and love beautiful things, (especially beautiful women). God wired us to admire and love the incredible beautiful creation of women, however as discussed in the previous chapter, this should be reserved for your Bride.

The internet is a powerful tool for both good and evil. It allows for such easy access to both graphic pornography as well as "soft" pornography.

We all know what graphic pornography is, but what is soft pornography.

For me it is things that include pictures like:

Sports Illustrated Swimsuit Edition
Lingerie League Football
NFL Cheerleader photos
Basically anything with scantily clad women that the world would consider "harmless" – This could be, TV, Cable, Movie, Internet, Book or Magazine.

I think of these as the "gateway" visuals that can lead to graphic pornography. They lead you away from visions of your Bride and provide you with unrealistic thoughts.

I will not go into the long story of my struggles with pornography except to say that I was first exposed to it in the 1st grade and as an impressionable teenager, my own father had an entire library that clouded my mind and judgment for years.

I find that my issues with pornography are exasperated when I am not in fellowship with God and my Bride. If I am lonely (on the road traveling) or angry (at God or my Bride), I know that is when I am most vulnerable

I learned a fine acronym that not only works here, but with anytime I am faced with making a decision. I should check myself and - HALT.

H – Hungry
A – Angry
L –Lonely
T - Tired

I find that I make really really bad decisions when I have three of these four attributes present (especially anything tied in with Hungry). Remembering to HALT has "saved my bacon" so many times! Full disclosure, I still fail sometimes and must seek God's forgiveness as well as forgiveness from others that I many have harmed.

Overall, knowing what can contribute to poor decision making has been very helpful for me.

Homework: Make HALT part of your vocabulary this week and imprint on your mind and heart. Share HALT with someone else this week as well.

Chapter 28

Beware of Social Networking with the Opposite sex!

We will use Facebook as our example of social network, but these thoughts apply to all social networking!

Remember that I am speaking to married men (and women) here.

This will be an incredibly short chapter (and I know some of you will disagree with me).

You do not need to be "friends" with members of the opposite sex (other than your close family members) on your social network!

If you are "friends" with other females –why? Work? School? Church? To what end and purpose?

Your Bride can be friends with the wife of your friends, but you should not! Is that a bit extreme, yes!

You should not be "friends" with that old girl friend from high school or college.

You have one and only one best friend and that is your BRIDE!

If you are making excuses right now about the female friends you have on Facebook, just ask yourself about the relationship you have with them and if that relationship would change if they were no longer your friend on Facebook.

I am fairly belligerent on this point for two reasons:

1. There are too many stories of men leaving their Bride and hooking up with that old flame

2. We just talked about guarding you "eye gates" and there are pictures on your "friends" sites that you do not need to view! It is one thing to view images of scantily clad women that you do not know, it is quite another level of temptation to view these pictures of people that you do know.

BTW – I do not have Facebook for these very reasons! I know what a knucklehead I am, and I don't need to add any fuel to my stupidity.

My Bride is my social network!

Homework: Take a really hard look at your social network and see if there is an opportunity to remove yourself from any temptation.

Chapter 29

Hold Hands

Do you remember when you first met your Bride and just holding her hand was special and exciting? Guess what, even if it not "special and exciting" after 10 years of marriage for you, it is still very special and exciting for her!

After those last couple of chapters, this is one of those easy chapters for you to read and follow.

When should you hold her hand? Every opportunity that you get!

Here are some suggestions where to hold her hands:

- Church – when you are listening to the music or preaching
- Weddings – remember she loves going to weddings
- Funerals – she will need to feel your strength and closeness
- On a date – remember the Bride of your Youth
- In bed at night – this is a sweet way to show your love in a non-verbal way
- On a walk – see next chapter

It is a small magical thing and can help encourage and brighten you Bride's day.

It's easy – just start doing it!

Homework: See how many times this week you can hold your Bride's hand.

Chapter 30

Walk with your Bride

This is another easy chapter. I had to learn this principle the hard way (meaning my Bride had to point it out to me).

I walk fast! I mean really fast!!! I am always in a hurry and a rush and walking fast is my modus operandi.

Unfortunately, my Bride walks slower than me.

So we might be walking across the parking lot to church and I would be 10 paces ahead of her (thinking that is was important to be fast and get that good seat) and unbeknownst to me, I was both frustrating and aggravating my Bride.

She pulled me aside and told me how it made her feel when I walked off and left her (I really had no clue). I was devastated that something that I took for granted could be so hurtful.

This was an easy fix guys.

If you are holding hand (see previous chapter), you will not walk ahead of you Bride. You kill two birds with one stone.

Beware that holding her hand is not an invitation to drag her along at a faster pace (although you can pick up the pace a little bit.)

If your Bride walks faster than you (I know several that do), then keep up! Start an exercise routine if you need to.

Again, this is easy stuff, but very powerful.

Just do it!

Homework: Take a walk with your Bride.

Chapter 31

True Intimacy is only Possible when her Emotional Bank is Full

Let's talk about money. When you put money in your savings account at the bank you expect to earn interest and get a return on your deposits. The more money you put in, the greater your return. I would also venture to say, that most men pay more attention to their bank accounts than the Bride's emotional account.

This same principle holds true with your Bride. When you make deposits into her emotional bank account you can expect a return on those deposits. There is a caveat though! The deposits must be real, sincere and timely. Just as if you were to deposit counterfeit money into your bank account it would get rejected and you would also most likely be in trouble, the same is true if your deposits into Bride's emotional account are counterfeit.

Here are some worthy suggestions for making deposits – some are easy and others are a bit tougher. I want to be clear, that the goal here is not manipulation, but edification! Your role is to build up your Bride continually.

I will break this up into three areas: Things to say, Things not to say, Things to Do,

Things to say:

- I love you!
- You look great today!
- I still want you!
- You are the only one for me!
- You are beautiful!

- I need you!
- You are doing a great job with _____ (you fill in the blank – kids, house, job etc)
- I am so glad you said YES, when I asked you to marry me!
- You complete me!
- Thank you for _____ (you fill in the blank)
- I am so grateful for you!
- You are my best friend!

Things not to say:

- You're not wearing that are you?
- Basically any negative comment about any part of her body is out of bounds. If she is overweight or saggy, she already knows this and does not need your comments.
- You are just like your mother (this of course being in the negative context)
- Comments about other women who have attributes that you Bride may not have (e.g. cleavage)
- Derogatory remarks of any kind (stupid, idiot, dummy, etc.)
- Do not make negative comments about the house or her cooking

Things to do:

- Clean up after yourself.
- Dress up for your date.
- Shave
- Clean the kitchen, bathroom, bedroom etc
- Do the dishes
- Cook supper and or Bring home supper
- Play with the kids
- Clean up the kids and put them to bed
- Don't be overly cruel or harsh to the children
- Listen, Listen, Listen
- Exercise and take care of yourself. Lead by example
- Keep your promises
- Take her out on a date
- Take her for a walk and hold her hand
- Put sticky notes all over her car that spell out "I Love You"

- Use your creativity to surprise her.

I know some of these are easy and some will require a modification to your behavior. Remember the more you do this, the more secure and loved you Bride will feel. Make sure it is sincere and timely. These are not things you do one time; these are lifetime habits and lessons.

Homework: now go do something to increase the investment in your Bride's emotional account.

Chapter 32

Nuggling

We just talked about real physical intimacy, what in the world is nuggling? It is a word we coined.

Here is a simple definition that guys will understand. Nuggling is snuggling without the intention of sex!

You see, most of the time, snuggling can and will lead to sex (which is a beautiful and wonderful thing).

But there are many times when your Bride just wants and needs to be held and not taken to the next level.

I cannot tell you how to nuggle, and I most certainly will not tell you how we nuggle, but I will tell you to make nuggling a part of your physical intimacy with your Bride.

She wants to know that you "want" her just for who she is in that moment and not because you have a sexual need or desire.

There is plenty of time to practice both!

<u>Homework</u>: If you cannot figure this one out by yourself, ask your Bride and she will tell you exactly how to nuggle! She already knows, remember we are the knuckleheads!

The Things you need to do and Remember

Chapter 33

Be aligned with your Bride on Rewards and Discipline for Kids

I cannot tell you how many times we have seen this issue create havoc in our friend's marriages. You cannot have two different sets of standards for rewards and discipline for your kids. There must be one "program" and everybody needs to be on the same page.

This is one area Debbie and I learned about early on with our kids (did I mention we have four of them). We set a standard for discipline that applied to all of our children. What we did was apply the rules of "D". If they crossed the line on any of the "D's", they knew they were going to be disciplined.

Here are the D's –

Disrespect

Disobedience

Dishonesty

We had decided early only that if and when the kids crossed the line in any of these areas, they would receive correction and discipline. They all fall back on biblical principles we follow for our lives

Disrespect –

Exodus 20:12 – "Honor your father and your mother, that your days may be prolonged in the land which the LORD *your God gives you.*

Disobedience -

Ephesians 6:1 – Children, obey your parents in the Lord, for this is right

Colossians 3:20 - Children, be obedient to your parents in all things, for this is well-pleasing to the Lord.

Dishonesty

Exodus 20:15 – You shall not steal

Exodus 20:16 – You shall not bear false witness against your neighbor

Proverbs 12:22 - Lying lips are an abomination to the LORD, but those who deal faithfully are his delight

Not only did we need to be aligned around what areas to discipline, we also had to be aligned around the type of discipline. I would direct you to James Dobson's books – Dare to Discipline and The New Dare to Discipline. These are excellent resources that both of you should read together.

It is so important to be aligned around the types and level of discipline, because if you are not, then there is the distinct possibility that you can drive a wedge into your marriage if your Bride thinks you are being overly harsh or cruel (because mama bear can be overly protective of her cubs).

This biggest mistake we see many people make is that they want to be friends with their children. The only problem with this sentiment is that we are not called to be friends; we are called to be their parents! Being a parent is supposed to be tough, hard and a marathon. Many times you will need to make hard decisions for your child, and if you are their friend, you would not be able to do this.

Are friendships important? Of course they are. But if you are honest, you know that friendship is much different than being a parent. Our kids do not need one more friend, they need someone to be the adult and make thoughtful and timely and sometimes tough decisions.

These tough decisions not only apply to discipline, they also apply to rewards as well. You must decide the type, level and amount of reward and stick to it. You cannot have one parent giving the kids $100 for cleaning their room and the other parent giving them a complement and pat on the back for cleaning their room. I know this is an extreme example, but the point it to decide together how you will reward your children.

Not having a game plan and thinking this through will only cause you headache and heartache.

Homework: If you are not aligned, then spend time talking through the issues and get aligned. It is never too late to start.

Chapter 34

Don't let the Kids Divide and Conquer

Kid are smarter than your think! They are masters at dividing and conquering. Military leaders could take lessons from most 6 year olds.

You have to shut this type of behavior down instantly or it will cause chaos in your life.

Here is a typical example in our house.

Jonathan will go to Debbie and ask if he can have a Popsicle. Debbie will tell him no and that he needs to eat lunch first. Jonathan will then approach me and ask if he can have a Popsicle. I of course do not know that Debbie has told him "no". If I tell him yes, then we have just reinforced the fact that he can go from one parent to the other and get what he wants (all four of our kids have tried this maneuver).

Debbie and I have a simple way for deal this behavior

Whenever one of them comes to us and asks for something, our automatic response is "What did your Dad/Mom say?" or "Did you already ask Dad/Mom?"

This puts them in the uncomfortable position of deciding to tell the truth or tell a lie. If they tell the truth, then they will not get the popsicle, but they also will not get disciplined. If they lie, they run the risk of getting caught (they almost always get caught) and then they have to deal with the consequences of that behavior. Remember the previous chapter about being aligned on discipline.

<u>Homework:</u> Don't let the kids divide and conquer! Have a plan with your Bride and stick to that plan.

Chapter 35

After the Glue Dries – Embrace the "Tragedies" of Life

Things are going to happen all the days you walk on this earth. Some will be good, some will be great and others will bring sadness, heartache or tears. This chapter is really about how to make lemonade out of lemons.

I use the word tragedies loosely here. I am not talking about life or death. I am talking about the stuff that happens and has the potential to be a great learning lesson and family bonding experience – if we choose to let it be. When you learn to embrace these tragedies, you will learn to live a full life and enjoy the things that come your way. If nothing else, these are the things we remember.

Here are some examples –

When my kids were younger we lived in Houston Texas and I worked about an hour from our house. I did not get to see the kids much, so Debbie would bring them down to the office and we would go to the park and eat lunch and play. One day we went to McDonalds and got Happy Meals and pies and went to the park. We enjoyed our lunch and left the pies for later. I took the kids to the swings and while we were away, some black birds came and ate our pies. The kids screamed and yelled at the black birds and were very sad. From that day forward, these were the apple pie eating birds. No matter where we went, when they saw those birds, they were the apple pie eating birds.

Hannah, David and I went camping and our tent leaked and we got soaked! Great memory!

We all went boating on the lake and got caught in a huge thunderstorm! Soaked and memorable!

We all went white water rafting and Jonathan fell out and we had to "rescue" him. He still talks about how awesome that was.

David dislocated his shoulder three times playing football. Painful, but memorable.

I remember when Debbie called me to say that David had dislocated his shoulder in practice and they were taking him to the hospital. After I found out he was ok, I asked if she got some good pictures. You see, we knew after he had healed that we would look back at the memory.

To be completely honest, this is something that we have had to grow into and learn, but as we gone through this kind of stuff, the lens we view it from is completely different.

Nobody ever remembers the perfect camping trip where nothing goes wrong. How boring! We remember when the squirrels got into our box of food and ate holes in everything.

I would never make light of life and death matter, but we seldom face those. We face these other little things every day.

Learn to embrace them (keep you camera or cell phone handy for photos), and I promise you will enjoy life just a little bit more.

> **Homework:** Start this week to have the right attitude towards these types of events and plan in advance how you will choose to react.

Chapter 36

Share your Dreams, Hopes, Desires and Goals

Life is zero fun without dreams, hopes and desires. It is even less fun if you don't have someone to share them with.

I can honestly say that the first person in this life that I want to share my hopes, dreams and desires with is my Bride! She is my biggest cheerleader and a constant encouragement.

In return, I want to be her biggest encourager and help her reach for her dreams as well.

Debbie and I sit down regularly and make our dream lists and compare notes on what we would like to do with our lives.   We talk about home improvements, our children's future, missions' trips and ministry opportunities, retirement, exercise and fitness goals. The point is, we are constantly sharing with one another.

Here are some of the dreams I shared with Debbie and she encouraged me to pursue them all!

- Start my own website – Done!

- Get my MBA – Done!

- Start my own Blog – Done!

- Learn how to backpack – Done!

- Write this book – working on it!

- Work on another book – working on it!

- Running and exercise goals – working on it!

I honestly would not have done most of these things without my Bride's support and understanding. She believes in me and I believe in her.

What are your dreams, hopes, desires and goals? Have you shared them with your Bride? If not, what is holding you back? Do you encourage your Bride? Do you support her dreams? Do you know what her dreams are?

When do we usually talk about this stuff? On our date nights. It is when we are relaxed and away from the kids and we can "come up for air".

Do you start to see how many of the principles that I have discussed throughout the book start to come together? It is not about only doing one or two of these things; it is about weaving it all together to form a seamless tapestry that is your life together.

Homework: - On your next date night, each of you bring your list of hopes, dreams, desires and goals. You might be surprised what is on your Bride's list. My guess is that many of the things on her list will have to do with people and relationships.

Lean on the Strength of your Spouse – you cannot do it all

We all think we can do it ourselves and don't need any help. We are wrong.

I know what my strengths are and when I use them to the extreme they can also be my weaknesses.

Here are some things I am not good at, but my Bride excels at! I need to lean into her strengths. She excels at:

- Reading people and situations (discernment)
- Mercy
- Only giving an answer when she is 100% certain she is correct
- Listening
- Algebra

I am a natural salesman, so for me being 100% correct is never completely necessary, I just need to be directionally correct and let the engineers and accountants solve for any deficiencies. ☺

However, in life outside of my job, that does not always work so well. I cannot tell you how many times Debbie has "saved my bacon". Of course it only took me about 5 years of marriage to figure this out.

Here is an easy example - before the advent of GPS and smartphones, we would be driving somewhere and I only mostly knew where we were going. I would be ready to make a right turn, and Debbie would say, no we need to go left. In my earlier years of marriage, pride would creep in and I would not listen to my Bride. Today, this is what I say – "are you sure?". If she says yes, then I make the left hand turn. You see, Debbie does not give an absolute answer unless she is 100% correct. She has proven herself again and again and now I know to trust her completely.

I know that I am not merciful but there are many situations where I need to rely on Debbie to provide the guidance and direction especially when it comes to our children and extended family.

The key is for you to know your strengths and weaknesses as well as your Brides strengths and weaknesses. Once you know these, don't let pride stand in the way of you leaning on your Bride.

I know many men, who think they are good at handling money, but they are not. Because of pride and control, they put their marriage and family in peril instead of trusting in the strength of their Bride.

Don't be one of those guys. Trust your Bride and lean on her strengths.

Homework: Write out all of the strengths of your Bride and keep the list handy. Figure out how you can best utilize her strengths to offset your weaknesses.

Chapter 38

Make your Bride your BEST FRIEND!!

Who is your best friend? If it is your Bride, you can stop reading and move on to the next chapter. Well done.

If it is not your Bride, I have to ask why? What is preventing your Bride from being your best friend?

You see, Debbie is my best friend! How do I define that:

- When something good happens to me – she is the first one I want to tell
- When something bad happens to me – she is the first one I want to tell
- If I had to choose one person to be stranded on an deserted island with – it would be her
- I want to spend as much time as I can with her
- I want to spend time getting to know her better (even after 20+ years of marriage)
- When she is hurting, I am hurting
- When she is joyful, I am joyful
- When she rejoices, I rejoice
- In sickness and in health – I want her by my side
- I want to do stuff that she likes to do

That does not mean I don't have other friends or that I don't do stuff without Debbie. It's just that I always choose her first!

They say the three rules of choosing a good business are:

- Location
- Location
- Location

The three rules for making your Bride your best friend are:

- Time with her
- Time with her
- Time with her

Sorry but this is no easy way to become best friends. You must spend time with each other doing stuff together.

If you are off with your buddies each weekend – hunting, fishing, camping, sports events, - you fill in the blank. Then when are you spending time with your Bride.

All the stuff listed above is good and fun stuff (I love that stuff!!). But not at the expense and complete exclusion of my Bride.

You have to find the balance that will work. I err on the side of doing more stuff with her! I love my buddies, but I live with my Bride! When times get tough – she will always be by my side.

What can you do this week, month, year to make your Bride a better friend? Will you commit with me to working towards making your Bride your best friend? I hope so.

Life is too short to not have a best friend that you live with each and every day.

Homework: Do something with your Bride this week. Create a memory

Chapter 39

Never stop Reading and Learning about Marriage and Family

Why have I read so many books? When I first got married I knew that I did not have any positive role models for what a husband or father should be. Therefore, I asked other wiser men for advice and books they would recommend I read. I took them at their word and started reading and researching how to be a better husband and father and applying those principles in my life (some successfully other not so much).

The fact that you are reading this book is a positive move in the right direction. As I said at the beginning of this book, I don't know how many of these thoughts are original, or how many came from books I have read. Below is a compilation of some of the better books I have read. (I love to read). There are some excellent books listed here and many I have not listed. The point is- your learning never ends.

Some of you might say that you do not like to read. I would challenge that assumption and say, that many people enjoy reading what is important to them. How much time do you spend reading the following subjects?

- Sports
- World/National/Local News
- Politics
- Hobbies

You read a lot more than you think! You just have to prioritize what you read and more importantly why you are reading. The objective is for you to grow and learn and be a better man in all aspects of your life.

If you were only going to read one book, read the first one at the top of the list. I have read it and re-read it many times! _If Only He Knew_ is a powerful book that will help you better understand your Bride.

If Only He Knew	- Gary Smalley
The 5 Love Languages	- Gary Chapman
Father's & Daughter's	- Jack & Jerry Schreur
The Language of Love	- Gary Smalley & John Trent
"Daddy's Home"	- Greg Johnson & Mike Yorkey
Hidden Keys of a Loving Lasting Marriage	- Gary Smalley
The Hidden Value of a Man	- Gary Smalley & John Trent
What Kids Need Most in a Dad	- Tim Hansel
Father's & Son's	- Jack & Jerry Schreur
Point Man	- Steve Farrar
Go the Distance	- John Trent
In the Grip of Grace	- Max Lucado
Love for a Lifetime	- Dr. James Dobson
Staying in Love for a Lifetime	- Ed Wheat M.D.
Dare to Discipline	- Dr. James Dobson
The New Dare to Discipline	- Dr. James Dobson
Straight Talk	- Dr. James Dobson
Beside Every Great Dad	- Swihart & Canfield
The Road Unseen	- Jerry Jenkins

Daddy's Home	- *Steve Schnur*
The Power of the Promise Kept	- *Many*
7 Promises of a Promise Keeper	- *Many*
Hedges	- *Jerry Jenkins*
Rookie Dad	- *Rick Epstein*
She Calls me Daddy	- *Wolgemuth*
Disciplines in Grace	- *Hughes*
Locking Arms	- *Weber*
4 Pillars of a Man	- *Weber*
Intended for Pleasure	- *Ed Wheat M.D.*
Life on the Edge	- *Dr. James Dobson*
Standing Tall	- *Farrar*
As Iron Sharpens Iron	- *Howard & William Hendricks*
Tender Warrior	- *Weber*
The 5 Habits of Smart Dads	- *Lewis*
Raising a Modern Day Knight	- *Lewis*
Outdoor Insights	- *Steve Chapman*
What a Difference a Daddy Makes	- *Lehman*
Who's in Charge Here	- *Barnes*
I Love You, But Why are We so Different?	- *Layhaye*
Dating Your Mate	- *Bundschuh & Gilbert*
Twice Pardoned	- *Morris*

The Strong Willed Child	*- Dr. James Dobson*
Putting Amazing Back into Grace	*- Horton*
The Nature of Spiritual Growth	*- Wesley*
How a Many Stands up for Christ	*- Gilbert*
In Search of Excellence	*- Peters et.al.*
A Passion for Excellence	*- Peters et.al.*
7 Habits of Highly Effective People	*- Covey*
Love is a Decision	*- Smalley & Trent*
The Power of Personal Integrity	*-Charles Dyer*

Homework: buy one of the above books and read it!

Chapter 40

Remember that LOVE is an Action and not a Feeling

Feelings come and go.

I feel hot, I feel cold, I feel angry, I feel lonely, I feel happy, I feel like a fool.

I cannot trust my feeling, because I allow so many things to impact them. If I am hungry and tired, then I am going to feel grouchy and not be very nice to be around. Love cannot and should not be placed in the same universe as feelings.

Love should be constant and unwavering. Like the North Star on a dark night. You should know it is always there in the same spot.

Love is an action. Love is something you choose to do even when you do not "feel" like it.

What are the actions of love? There is a great book written by Gary Chapman on *The 5 Love Languages* that I highly recommend you read. It talks about the different love languages each person has:

- **Words of Affirmation**
  These are your spoken or written words to your Bride.

I will write Debbie notes and will leave them on the coffee maker or put them in her car. I will send her a text in the middle of the day just to say I love you and you are a great mother and friend.

- **Quality Time**
  Time together just you and your Bride.

These are our date nights and time together on weekends away from the kids. Sometimes it is just the early morning quiet before the kids begin to stir.

- **Gifts**
  I don't know to many Brides who do not like appropriate, well timed gifts

Debbie does not really like jewelry, but she does love gifts for the house or practical things that make her life easier. She also likes tickets to Broadway shows (which is a 'twofer" because it is a gift and quality time)

- **Acts of Service**
  Cleaning the kitchen, fixing her coffee, mowing the grass, putting the kids to bed

Debbie loves nothing better than to wake up to a clean kitchen. It is a small thing to load and unload the dishwasher and see the joy that it brings to her heart.

- **Physical Touch**
  This is holding her hand, a gentle back rub or just stoking her hair.

This is as simple as holding Debbie's hand when we are in public.

If you cannot figure out your Bride's love language, ask her. I guarantee she will let you know. Then remember it is not enough to know; now you must act on that knowledge.

Forget the feelings and move towards action. Especially when you do not feel like loving your Bride. Choose a love language and love her anyway.

<u>Homework:</u> Go buy this book, read it and follow the examples and instructions. It is a powerful book.

Chapter 41

Keep your Promises

I remember when the Promise Keepers came out and how it swept that nation and rallied men to be more committed to their Bride and their children. It was an awesome experience and provided me with a new focus to be the husband and father I needed to be.

Where do we start with our promises? Let's start with our Bride and the ultimate promise we all made the day we stood before our family and friends and traded wedding vows.

Traditional Wedding Vows 1:

I, Paul, take you Debbie, to be my Bride, to have and to hold from this day forward, for better or for worse, for richer, for poorer, in sickness and in health, to love and to cherish; from this day forward until death do us part.

Traditional Wedding Vows 2:

I, Paul, take you, Debbie, to be my Bride, my constant friend, my faithful partner and my love from this day forward. In the presence of God, our family and friends, I offer you my solemn vow to be your faithful partner in sickness and in health, in good times and in bad, and in joy as well as in sorrow. I promise to love you unconditionally, to support you in your goals, to honor and respect you, to laugh with you and cry with you, and to cherish you for as long as we both shall live.

Traditional Wedding Vows 3 (traditional civil ceremony vows):

Debbie, I take you to be my lawfully wedded wife. Before these witnesses I vow to love you and care for you as long as we both shall live. I take you with all your faults and your strengths as I offer myself to you with my faults and strengths. I will help you when you need help, and I will turn to you when I need help. I choose you as the person with whom I will spend my life.

Traditional Wedding Vows 4:

I, Paul, take you, Debbie, to be my beloved Bride, to have and to hold you, to honor you, to treasure you, to be at your side in sorrow and in joy, in the good times, and in the bad, and to love and cherish you always. I promise you this from my heart, for all the days of my life.

Let's take a full stop right here. Do you remember this time? Do you remember your promise? Take a few minutes to reflect on that special time and recommit yourself to your Bride.

These of course are some of the most important promises in our life, but what about all those other small promises we make each day and week.

- I promise to clean the garage out this weekend
- I promise to take the kids to the park
- I promise to take you on a date
- I promise to stop looking a pornography
- I promise put the lid down on the toilet
- I promise to make it to your – ball game, musical, dance recital, etc.

You see we make all kinds of promises each day and our Bride and our children are looking to us to see if we will keep those promises.

Every time you keep a promise you reinforce the value of that person to you. And conversely, you diminish their value when you do not keep your promise. Ultimately this is about trust! Can your family trust you and believe you are a man of your word.

Trust is such a foundational element of all relationships, that when you do not keep your promises, you are tearing down the foundation you are standing upon.

Homework: what promise have you broken that you can work on this week? Ask forgiveness and create a new path for the promises you will keep.

Chapter 42

Do not Threaten Divorce or Leaving.

I just heard the saddest news yesterday. A young couple we know is getting a divorce. We knew these kids from the time they were in middle school, until they got married only 9 years ago. They have two children, she is pregnant and he is leaving her. His reason? It's just not fun anymore.

I looked up the antonyms for FUN

annoying, boring, tiring, unfunny, chore, task, vocation, work, disagreeable, displeasing, unenjoyably, unhappy, unpleasant, unsatisfying

These antonyms are his true feeling and what he meant to say was - "this marriage and family thing is tough, hard work and I just might have to sacrifice some of myself to make this work". When the going gets tough – the boys leave and the men stay! This does separate the men from the boys.

Needless to say, this young lady is devastated.

I have heard it said time and time again that the number one desire for our Bride's is security. What do they want to be secure in?

- The knowledge of your love. It is unconditional and unwavering
- The knowledge that you will never leave – remember the vows - in sickness and in health
- The knowledge of your work ethic and helping to provide for your family
- The knowledge the you are keeping your hands and lips to yourself, your eyes and mind on her and your feet on a path that always leads home

You tear down those walls of security when you threaten to leave or threaten divorce. Don't be that kind of guy.

I have never threatened to leave my Bride nor has divorce even been a subject of conversation (other than to lament it happening to others). I so want all of you to have the same kind of relationship with your Bride that I have with mine.

Is marriage tough – sure it is! Is my Bride perfect (I know I should say yes right here, but I need to be truthful) – no! Am I perfect – a resounding NO! So you have two imperfect people from different backgrounds coming together as ONE.   Yes it can be tough, but it is also the second most incredible thing that has ever impacted my life. I am a better man, husband and father because of my Bride.   I really am only half a person without her.

BTW – the most important thing that impacted my life?   The day I trusted Jesus Christ as my personal Lord and Savior.   I was a broken, wretched person before I knew Christ as my Savior. My own family said that I would be dead or in jail by the time I was 16 years old.   I was the kind of person that you told you kids never to hang out with and to stay away from.

I had never been to church or heard the Good News of the gospel, but a high school friend offered to take me to a revival at the high school one night, and I asked Christ to forgive me of my sins and I put my trust in Him as my personal Lord and Savior.   He is the other reason that I am a better man, husband, and father.

Christ changed my path and the trajectory of my life.   If you don't know him today, here are some bible verses to help you understand what God can do for you:

Romans 3:23 – _for all have sinned and fall short of the glory of God_

Romans 6:23 – _For the wages of sin is death, but the free gift of God is eternal life in Christ Jesus our Lord._

Romans 5:8 – _But God demonstrates His own love toward us, in that while we were yet sinners, Christ died for us._

Romans 10:9-10 – _that if you confess with your mouth Jesus as Lord, and believe in your heart that God raised Him from the dead, you will be saved; [10] for with the heart a person believes, resulting in righteousness, and with the mouth he confesses, resulting in salvation_

John 14:6 – _Jesus said to him, "I am the way, and the truth, and the life. No one comes to the Father except through me._

John 3:16 – _"For God so loved the world, that He gave His only begotten Son, that whoever believes in Him shall not perish, but have eternal life._

Ephesians 2:8-9 – _For by grace you have been saved through faith; and that not of yourselves, it is the gift of God; [9] not as a result of works, so that no one may boast._

Put your faith and trust in Christ today and let Him change your path and trajectory.

Here is a final thought. Where do your kids get security? From the knowledge that mom and dad are always going to be together, because when you leave, you don't just leave your Bride, you are leaving your children as well.

Homework: Make a commitment today to see your marriage through until the end. When the going gets tough, the men step up!

Chapter 43

Be a Dream-maker, not a Dream-taker

I would like to think this is one of the few original ideas I have in this book (including Flowers on Tuesday).

I am really good at saying NO. As a matter of fact, I have it down to a science. I don't even need to hear an entire question and I can already determine that I will say NO.

You see, many times when I was saying NO, it was because of selfish reasons on my part, not because of some logical or well thought out reason.

This is mostly written from the context as a father, as opposed to being a husband, but what I have found is that when I am being a dream-maker for my children, it draws me closer to my Bride and builds our relationship even more.

This principle of being a dream-maker took me a really long time to learn and even longer to make a part of "who I am". Today it is such an ingrained part of my thought process, that I automatically process questions and requests through this filter. That does not mean there will not be any more NO's (there are still plenty of them). But this filter allows me to view the request from their perspective and ask myself if the NO is motivated by my own selfishness.

You see, being a dream-maker means investing my time, talents and treasures (do you see the recurring theme in this book?) I am a selfish person when it comes to these three areas of my life and it is only by the Grace of God and an intentional focus that allows me not to fail all the time.

My Bride taught me a very important lesson when it comes to our children. I would complain about being at one of their activities and how much time it was taking. She looked at me and said "don't wish this time away. It will be gone soon enough". Wow, it pierced my heart because she was SOOOO right!! We use this line with each other when one of us not particularly happy with an activity or situation.

Being a dream-maker does not always involve lots of time and money, however sometimes it will. Each family will have to determine how much to invest, but I would only ask you to consider how you balance this across all of your children and your Bride. Also, make sure it is their dream and not yours! We have too many friends and family members who are trying to live vicariously through their children. Spending every weekend on one person's activity is not balance and it precludes you from being a dream-maker for others.

Here are some of the things we have done to be dream-makers:

- When my two oldest kids turned 18, they wanted to jump out of a perfectly good airplane (with parachutes of course). Crazy - maybe, risk involved – sure, cost time and treasure – you bet. Dream for them – priceless.
- Learn Chinese – spending a summer in China to learn the language like a native
- Spend a year in Ireland as a missionary before going to college
- Having my daughter pilot a plane when she turned 15
- Being a musician and creating a band
- Singing in choir and musicals
- Becoming an Eagle Scout
- Going to Ecuador on a missions trip
- Going to Mall of America with my both my daughters when they turned 10
- Going to Lego Land with my youngest son when he was 9. His Dream was to fly on a plane (all of his brothers and sisters had) and he was a Lego fanatic.
- Building a tree house
- Visiting University campus
- Taking Bride to NYC to see Broadway plays

To be a dream-maker, you have to spend time with your family to understand what their dreams are and which ones are real and which are just whimsy. You do not need to say yes to all of them, but try to have more yes's than no's.

One final thought. With my older kids I like to test whether or not their idea is a true dream or just whimsy.

When they come to me with an idea and it will cost money and time, I ask them if they are willing to "put skin in the game". Meaning, how much money are they going to invest. If they are willing to invest their own money, then I know it is serious. Once I know they are serious, then I will meet them half way from a financial perspective. If a dream is going to cost $1,000, then they have to come up with $500 and I will match them with $500. They both have had jobs since they were 16 (now they are 20 and 21) and earn enough money to contribute to their dreams (I also look for ways to give them more without them knowing).

I can honestly say it is a lot more fun being a dream-maker!

Homework: – whose dream can you fulfill today? Think of one that will not cost you much money, but will require an investment of your time.

I promise you will have fun with this one!

.

Chapter 44

Just do it! Don't wait to get Motivated

Nike – Just do it! What a fantastic advertising line. Succinct and spot on!

You have been reading a lot about actions you need to take to have a more fulfilled and successful marriage and family.

You cannot wait to get motivated. Why? Because motivation is a feeling and you cannot trust your feeling to determine what you need to do. You now know what you need to do, you cannot wait upon a feeling to determine your next steps.

There are going to be days when you are not motivated, yet you still need to love your Bride and serve her.

What you will discover is that when you do those things that you know to do, even when you are not motivated, you will be much more proud of yourself and the result. It is like a runner who has committed to running every day for a year. There is no way he is motivated 365 days to run. It is on those days when he is not motivated to run, but he runs anyway, those are the break through days. That is when the runner starts to separate himself from the rest of the pack and go from ordinary to extraordinary. Choose to be extraordinary.

Homework: Make a list of things that you know you need to do, but have been waiting to get motivated. Determine in your mind (the greatest distance traveled), that you will be that guy who will push through and Just Do It. You will not wait to be motivated.

I know you can do it. It is just a matter of investment on your part. Are you willing to take the challenge and make the investment?

Chapter 45

We Practice what we Believe, all the rest is just Talk

This will be another one of those short chapters.

So you say you are a great father, husband and friend. I'm from Missouri – you have to show me.

Show me how you spend your time – look at your calendar for the past 3 months. Where have you spent your time?

- What % of your time went to your Bride? I'm not talking about falling asleep each night. Let's be honest. How much one-on-one time did she get in the last three months

Show me how you spend your money – look at your credit/debit card statement, you bank accounts and investment accounts. Where did you spend your money these past three months?

- What % of your money went to your Bride? I'm not talking groceries or beauty products here. Let's be honest. How much money did you invest in the last three months building a better relationship with your Bride?

My desire if for you to start building habits that reinforce your relationship with your Bride. The only way to do that is to invest time and money. Both are limited resources and will require you to determine how you will allocate them for maximum benefit for your marriage.

BTW – if you are already doing all of this. Congratulations. Now, how can you take it to the next level?

Use your talents to be creative and take you relationship to new heights.

You will not impress your Bride with your words; you will impress her with your actions.

Homework – break out your calendar and see how much time your Bride got in the past 3 months. Now think of ways to increase that amount of time.

Chapter 46

You cannot Change her!

I know this will come as a shock to many of you, but you cannot change your Bride! Some of you even now are trying to change her. Stop. It is not possible.

It is not possible to change you Bride, but what you can do is pray for your Bride and ask God to change her. It is not your duty or responsibility to change her, but it is your duty and responsibility to pray for her and lift her up to the Lord.

Well if you cannot change her, then what should you do (besides praying for her)?

You can change yourself! I have heard it said this way.

Draw a circle in the dirt about 2 feet in diameter, step into the circle. Now you need to change everybody in that circle! ☺

Things that you can change that will have an impact on your Bride

- She is not friendly – you become more friendly
- She has a bad attitude – you have a good attitude
- She does dress up – you dress up
- She does not pick up after herself – make sure your pick up after yourself
- Her cooking is not that great – you start cooking
- She is not a hard worker – you become a harder worker
- She is not good with the kids – you become the best father there is
- She talks to much – you become the best listener
- She does not show mercy – you become more merciful
- She is not romantic – you become Don Juan

I like this saying – "Be what you want others to become"

The bible also talks about not pointing out the splinter in someone else's eye, when you have a plank in yours. Meaning, they will not listen to you when they know you have faults in your life.

Stop trying to change your Bride and focus on changing yourself. Both of you will be better off in the long run.

Homework: start today praying for your Bride and then make the changes you need in your own life.

Chapter 47

Be Intentional

What do I mean by Intentional – I mean deliberate. Here are the synonyms

advised, aforethought, calculated, considered, designed, done on purpose, intended, meant, meditated, planned, prearranged, premeditated, proposed, purposed, studied, unforced, voluntary, willful, willing, witting

I tell my kids all the time – "Have a plan and then work your plan".

We have talked about a lot of things in this book. If you are going to make these principles a reality in your life, then you must be intentional, you must have a plan.

What do I mean? Can you give us some examples? Glad you asked

I know that I want to take my Bride on some special dates next year (today is February 5th, 2013 and I am already thinking about 2014). I just received a brochure in the mail about the new Broadway season at the Fox Theatre for next year. Valentine's Day is just around the corner, so I am going to kill two birds with one stone. I will purchase the Broadway series of tickets (6 shows), and give them to her on Valentine's Day. I have now been intentional about dating my Bride into the next year and doing something she absolutely loves.

I want to take my daughters out on "daddy dates". I put those in my calendar and schedule the time. I want to go hunting with my youngest son.- booked it in the calendar. My oldest son loves movies; each month I want to take him to a new release and enjoy the time together (recently saw The Hobbit at Midnight showing). My oldest daughter loves to run (so do I), so we plan runs and exercise together.

With these most important relationships, you cannot go through life haphazardly. You must be intentional and you must have plan.

Here are some thought starters

- If you don't have a calendar or don't use one – start today. You can use the one on your phone, computer or tablet, or you can just buy an old fashioned paper calendar/day timer
- Buy seasons tickets to something – shows, games, - whatever you can enjoy together
- Buy movie passes in advance – go ahead and buy six months' worth – now you are committed
- Plan that weekend get-away that will happen 6 months from now
- Get up every morning and make her coffee
- Hire a maid service to come clean the house

This is going to take in investment from you! You will need to invest your time, talents and treasure towards being intentional.

Homework: pick one thing today that you can do to be more intentional in your life.

How we Spend our Money

Chapter 48

Set Financial Goals and a Budget Together

I had mentioned earlier in the book that there were three key things that caused friction in a marriage:

- Money
- Children
- Intimacy

One of the biggest points of contention in a marriage is about how the money will be spent.

This chapter is all about the money. However, unlike Jerry McGuire, I am not going to "show you the money", I am going to show you how to avoid conflict with the money.

Let me start by saying that I am a huge fan of Dave Ramsey, so if you know the principles that he shares and what he believes, then a lot of this material will seem very familiar. If you do not know Dave Ramsey, I would highly encourage you to listen to his radio show and read his books. It is very easy and practical advice.

Setting goals may be new for some of you and for other it is old hat. Many of you set goals in your life for many things but not how you are going to spend your money. Here are some common goals people set:

Lose 10 lbs. in 2 weeks
Learn a new language
Run a marathon

You see we all have goals, but many times they are only mental or perhaps verbal, but seldom are they actually written down. I am going to encourage you to use the SMART method for setting your financial goals.

S = specific
M = measurable
A= actionable
R= realistic
T = time bound (and or time limit)

In addition to setting SMART goals you are much more likely to complete your goals if they are written down.

With that said, let's talk about the money!

Since you don't want money to be a point of contention or problem in your marriage, setting these goals together is key. You must be completely aligned on the goals and hold each other accountable to keeping them.

When Debbie and I got married, we brought into the marriage two very different philosophies on money. She was a spender and I was a saver. She had grown up in a very safe and comfortable middle class life style and I had grown up rather poor and in distress at times.

We knew we would need to reconcile our differences or else they could tear us apart.

We sat down and talked about what was important in our lives and where we wanted to invest our money. This did not happen overnight and it has evolved throughout our marriage, but the key is that we are aligned and in agreement on these overarching goals.

Here are the big buckets that we use to classify the money (a Dave Ramsey principle is to know where each and every dollar is going. I am not going to get that specific; I want you to understand the concept of having the goals and gaining alignment with your Bride)

- Charity/Gifts
- Retirement
- School & College
- Emergency Funds

- Vacation

You see, if you don't have a goal and plans, then money will just slip through your hands and this will ultimately lead to conflict (because bills will not get paid, dreams will not be made, and stress will enter your life)

I want to juxtapose examples of non-smart goals and SMART goals. We will assume this family makes $60,000 per year and has one son who is 8 years old

Non-smart goal

We want to save money for college.

While this may sound good, it is too vague, not measurable, not time-bound.

SMART goal

We want to save $20,000 over the next 10 years for our son's college expenses. We will save $167 each month starting next month and invest the money in a 529 savings plan.

This goal meets all of the criteria to be a SMART goal

Specific – Money for son's college into a 529 plan
Measurable - $20,000 (or $167 each month)
Actionable – start next month
Reasonable – on a monthly basis this is about 3.3% of their income.
Time-bound – each month for the next 10 years

The items that were listed at the beginning of the chapter were specific things to save for and setting the goals to put money away. Those are typically longer term things.

For those more immediate needs, you need to have a family "operating" budget. These are the day to day, week to week recurring items in your life. Each of these should have a specific amount allocated and then you never spend more than that amount. If you put aside $400 per month for groceries, then when the $400 is spent for that month you stop buying groceries. It will force you to consider how each dollar is spent.

We use Dave Ramsey's method of having an envelope with cash money. We get paid every two weeks and we replenish the money in each envelope. If you stick with it, you literally cannot spend more than you make. It works!

- Household (the day to day operating expenses – utilities, food, cleaning supplies, repairs etc.)
- Auto – (insurance, gas, taxes and maintenance)
- Entertainment
- Tithe
- Mortgage

Setting up a budget is somewhat easier than the goals, because you have the past history of what you have spent. You know about how much you spend on utilities each month.

When you have this budget figured out, then you know how much is left over for the bigger goals in your life.

Again, I encourage you to visit www.daveramsey.com and look under the tools folder. You will find more than enough resources to help you.

Homework: what is the one financial area of your life that is out of control? Try to tackle that area together as a team. Or try setting up your family budget.

Chapter 49

Don't have Separate Financial Accounts

This is the one that trips up so many people. In the end, it is about control and selfishness.

When both spouses are working, there can be the tendency to have "his money" and "her money". When you got married, you became ONE entity. There is no more "this is mine and that is yours". Everything is now OURS.

You have to be fully committed in your marriage and this includes money and finances. There has to be complete trust between the two of you on how and when the money is spent (see previous chapter). When you are aligned on those goals, there is no need for separate financial accounts. Everything is shared and everything is combined (both the risk and the reward).

You see, if you have a separate account, then there is the tendency to want to spend that money on your own wants and needs. You start to think, well I earned it and now I can spend it any way I like.

For many people it is just as much a matter of control as it is selfishness. Some cannot give us even the tiniest amount of control in their life.

Ask yourself, what harm can come from only having one checking account? Or conversely, why do you have separate checking accounts? Are you hiding purchases from your spouse? Does your Bride have full visibility into your spending?

Debbie and I had gotten this advice early on in our marriage and I cannot begin to tell you how helpful it was. We have NEVER argued about whose money is whose. We have always viewed it as our money. Having this agreement and thought process has saved us a lot of headache and heartache. You see, when it is OUR money then we both have a vested interest in doing what is right for OUR family.

Debbie's grandmother was the type of woman who was always in control! She had her own job, her own money and that was that! Early in our marriage she tried to get Debbie to open her own checking account and she promised to put money in the account for Debbie to spend on herself. Debbie refused and said we did not keep things separate from one another, and if she wanted to give her a gift then she could just send a check or money. Needless to say this did not go over very well for a number of years, but in the end, Debbie held her ground and her grandmother would just give her gifts to spend on herself (which is perfectly fine).

The point is that Debbie and I are as aligned on this as we are on all of the other key areas of our life. We have never let finances become a wedge that can cause frustration, anxiety, fear or resentment. There may be some financial advisor out there that will tell you it does not make sense, but I am telling you from the perspective of someone who has been very happily married for 20+ years – it works!

Homework: if you have separate accounts, have a healthy discussion as to why and then close one of them out and combine your lives in this area. And the two shall become one!

Chapter 50

Avoid debt – Especially Credit Card Debt

Boy is this chapter going to make some of you uncomfortable!

I had told you earlier in the book about Debbie being a spender and me being a saver. When we first got married, Debbie had a car payment and she owned a house. Her car payment was $400 per month (at 23% interest) and her house payment was $1,200 per month (at 14% interest). Her take home pay was not much more than these combined payments.

The first thing we did was pay her car off ($8,000). The second thing we did was refinance the mortgage to 9% (which was a fantastic rate back in the day). From that day until this, we have been aligned on our hatred of debt and the problems it brings.

The only debt that we have in our lives is the mortgage on our house. We have a 15 year loan and we cannot wait to pay it off!

Most all of the debt that people accrue is self-imposed! Yes I know there may be some of you with special circumstances, but you are a very small percentage of the population. The vast majority of people put themselves into debt and sometimes it is unsustainable debt.

Avoid credit cards at all costs! They are an avenue of easy money and very few people can control them. Some will say – I use them for points or rewards or cash back and I pay the bill in full each month. Congratulations, you are a very small percent of the population. You still have the issue of controlling your spending, because unless you keep close watch over every receipt, you cannot know what you have spent each month until the bill comes. With the cash method, you can never over spend. However, the vast majority of people make credit card payment each month and it is killing them. Cut up your cards and start spending cash instead.

How do we avoid debt?

We don't spend more than we make! We pay cash! When the cash is gone, the spending stops. You probably say – that is too simple. Yep! **Simple works**. It does not take a rocket scientist (no offense to rocket scientist) to figure this out.

You might say, what about cars?? We buy good used cars for about $5,000 to $6,000 in cash. They are usually about 10 years old and will require more maintenance. However, even if I spend $1,000 per year fixing them (which has never happened) this would only equate to $83 per month. The key is having an emergency fund available (which we do) to pay for any repair. Then you don't sweat driving an older car. Is there some risk involved? Sure there is. I am no mechanic, but I do have several good guides that I have used over the years that keep us away from junkers. Also, we invest in AAA program that will give us peace of mind if we need roadside service or towing.

You see, we would rather have the risk of breakdown (which rarely happens anyway) than have the debt hanging over our heads.

According to Experian, the average new car payment is $452 per month and the average used car payment is $354 per month. That means most people are paying between $4,200 and $5,400 per year on car payments. If you spent $2,000 per year on repairs, you would still be ahead of the game!

What about college? We saved money and are paying cash! Our kids also have jobs and pay for all of their own expenses (car, gas, insurance, cell phone, cloths, eating out etc). The best gift we can give our children is to have them graduate with no debt! Is it tough? Yes. Do we make sacrifices? Yes.

I pack a peanut butter and jelly sandwich to work every day! I don't eat out (except on a date with my Bride). Debbie shops at the thrift store for most of our cloths (you would be amazed at the bargains you can get).

Debt owns most people! It dictates their life and what they can and cannot do. They do not control the money the money controls them.

We hate debt with a passion! You need to hate it as well! Take control your finances and eliminate one of the key sources of conflict in a marriage.

Homework: go to www.daveramsey.com and start using those resources. They work!

Final Thoughts

Chapter 51

When you Don't Know What to do, do What you Know to do:

Ok, so here we are at the end. You have read through all the chapters and you are applying these principles in your life. It has been a lot of work, but I know you will be pleased with the results and your investment in time and energy will produce the kind of relationships that you will be proud of.

However, if you are like me, you are not going to remember all of these principles (at least not the first time through). I have read and re-read some of the books I talked early many, many times. It is a never ending process. You will not come to the end of your learning or growing. Learning is a lifelong process.

There will be some stressful times when you don't have time to think and you will be reacting. When those times come and you do not know what to do, do these things and you can almost never go wrong.

- Hold Her - (not intimate – but comforting)

- Hear Her - (listen to her without trying to solve)

- Help Her - (help her with those things that are causing the stress)

- Heal Her - (use soothing words of comfort to heal her broken spirit)

- Hoist Her – (lift her to the Lord in prayer)

I can promise you that it is not a question of if you will have times of crisis and stress. You will have times of crisis and stress and that is when your Bride will need you the most. This is the time to step up and be the man that she so richly deserves.

Homework: you have to be intentional about preparing for crisis and stress. Memorize those things you should do, so you are prepared when the crisis or stress comes.

One chapter to go and you are done!

p.s. – I want to give credit to Junior Hill who preached a message many years ago entitled "What to do when you do not know what to do". That message has spoken to me so deeply and is an ingrained part of my thinking

.

Chapter 52

Time Alone

This might seem like an odd chapter to add to the book, but it really is an essential principle it you want to grow and have the best possible relationship with your Bride and family.

What do I mean by time alone? Do I really mean to be alone, by yourself? Yes that is exactly what I mean.

While this whole book has been focused on building your relationship with others, we have not focused on you. You need to be taking care of yourself. This means physically, mentally, emotionally and most important spiritually.

Time alone is an opportunity to do all of these things.

For me, time alone is critical to refresh and renew myself and prepare me to be a better father, husband and friend. Here is how I use my time alone on a weekly basis.

<u>Spiritually</u> – I have my own time of bible study and prayer. I especially enjoy reading the proverbs and never grow tired of the wisdom. It is a time for me to reflect on my own relationship with Christ and the areas I need forgiveness and improvement. It is also the time I lift up my Bride and children to the Lord.

<u>Physically</u> – I know I need to take care of my body so that I can continue to be the provider and protector of my family. I have always enjoyed running, biking and swimming. For me these are almost always solitary pursuits and it allows me to release stress and do something that makes me feel good about myself. Invariably, it is also a good time of thought and reflection (especially when I am swimming). I find, the quiet of the pool very good for thoughts, ideas and prayer.

Mentally – I love reading, but with a large family and all the events of life swirling around each week, this is a tough pursuit. However, when I can, I get a good book, jump in the tub and soak for a good long time and read.   My family knows this is "my time" and they are gracious enough to give me this time to refresh myself.

Invariably I am a much better person throughout the day and week when I have my "alone" time. I actually schedule it in my weekly calendar and make it a priority.

While Jesus was here, he was always surrounded by his disciples or a crowd. But there are many example of time he slipped away to be alone and pray.   It is a good example for all of us to follow.

Mark 1:35

In the early morning, while it was still dark, Jesus got up, left *the house*, and went away to a secluded place, and was praying there.

Mark 6:45-46

Immediately Jesus made His disciples get into the boat and go ahead of Him to the other side to Bethsaida, while He Himself was sending the crowd away. [46] After bidding them farewell, He left for the mountain to pray.

Mark 14:32-34

They came to a place named Gethsemane; and He said to His disciples, "Sit here until I have prayed." [33] And He took with Him Peter and James and John, and began to be very distressed and troubled. [34] And He said to them, "My soul is deeply grieved to the point of death; remain here and keep watch."

Luke 4:42

When day came, Jesus left and went to a secluded place; and the crowds were searching for Him, and came to Him and tried to keep Him from going away from them.

Luke 5:16

But Jesus Himself would often slip away to the wilderness and pray.

Luke 6:12

It was at this time that He went off to the mountain to pray, and He spent the whole night in prayer to God.

Homework: do you have time alone? If not, look at your calendar and schedule some alone time. It does not have to be a lot of time, but you need to start this week.

Seek Wise Counsel

I would be remiss if I did not offer the advice for you to seek wise counsel. As a young man, I would seek out some of the men in my church who had been married for 25-30+ years and ask them questions about marriage and family. They had "been there, do that" and yes, many of them did have the t-shirt as well. It was valuable for me, because I did not have good role models growing up.

If you were lucky enough to have had good role models growing up, then seek wise counsel from them. If you did not have a good role model in your father, grandfather or uncles, then I would encourage you to seek out wise men from your church.

Offer to meet them from breakfast, lunch, or dinner and ask for their advice.

When people ask me about prayer requests, invariable I always ask for wisdom. Wisdom comes from God and can help me with every decision and action in my life. The Bible is my guide and compass for navigating the turbulent waters of this world and Christ is the foundation upon which my house is built! I give all the honor and glory and praise to God.

My final word for you is to point you to the bible and see what it says about seeking wise counsel and being wise.

James 1:5

But if any of you lacks wisdom, let him ask of God, who gives to all generously and without reproach, and it will be given to him.

Ephesians 5:15-17

Therefore be careful how you walk, not as unwise men but as wise, [16] making the most of your time, because the days are evil. [17] So then do not be foolish, but understand what the will of the Lord is.

James 3:17

But the wisdom from above is first pure, then peaceable, gentle, reasonable, full of mercy and good fruits, unwavering, without hypocrisy.

Proverbs 12:15
The way of a fool is right in his own eyes,
But a wise man is he who listens to counsel.

Proverbs 11:14

Where there is no guidance the people fall,
But in abundance of counselors there is victory.

Proverbs 19:20-21
Listen to counsel and accept discipline,
That you may be wise the rest of your days.
21 Many plans are in a man's heart,
But the counsel of the LORD will stand

Proverbs 24:3-7

By wisdom a house is built,
And by understanding it is established;
4 And by knowledge the rooms are filled
With all precious and pleasant riches.

5 A wise man is strong,
And a man of knowledge increases power.
6 For by wise guidance you will wage war,
And in abundance of counselors there is victory.

7 Wisdom is too exalted for a fool,
He does not open his mouth in the gate.

Proverbs 15:22

Without consultation, plans are frustrated,
But with many counselors they succeed.

Hebrews 4:12
For the word of God is living and active and sharper than any two-edged sword, and piercing as far as the division of soul and spirit, of both joints and marrow, and able to judge the thoughts and intentions of the heart.

Proverbs 1:7

The fear of the LORD is the beginning of knowledge;
Fools despise wisdom and instruction.

Psalm 1:1-6

How blessed is the man who does not walk in the counsel of the wicked,
Nor stand in the path of sinners,
Nor sit in the seat of scoffers!
2 But his delight is in the law of the LORD,
And in His law he meditates day and night.
3 He will be like a tree firmly planted by streams of water,
Which yields its fruit in its season
And its leaf does not wither;
And in whatever he does, he prospers.

4 The wicked are not so,
But they are like chaff which the wind drives away.
5 Therefore the wicked will not stand in the judgment,
Nor sinners in the assembly of the righteous.
6 For the LORD knows the way of the righteous,
But the way of the wicked will perish.

Proverbs 1:5
A wise man will hear and increase in learning,
And a man of understanding will acquire wise counsel,

Proverbs 13:10

Through insolence comes nothing but strife,
But wisdom is with those who receive counsel.

Proverbs 20:18
Prepare plans by consultation,
And make war by wise guidance.

Proverbs 28:26
He who trusts in his own heart is a fool,
But he who walks wisely will be delivered.

James 3:17-18

But the wisdom from above is first pure, then peaceable, gentle, reasonable, full of mercy and good fruits, unwavering, without hypocrisy. [18] And the seed whose fruit is righteousness is sown in peace by those who make peace.

Proverbs 20:15

There is gold, and an abundance of jewels;
But the lips of knowledge are a more precious thing.

I love the book of Proverbs and encourage you to read it as often as possible. There are 31 chapters, so it makes it very easy to read one chapter each day and make this your devotional. I have been doing this for years and never grow tired of the wisdom and insight I gain from reading Proverbs.

Homework: Seek out a handful of family members or friends who can be that wise counsel for you.

You made it to the end. Congratulations! It is my hope and prayer that this book has been beneficial to you and your family (especially your Bride).

Thank you so much for taking the time to read the entire book. Please take a moment to review this book on the website where you purchased it.

You can find additional information at: www.ILYNMW.com

Made in the USA
Middletown, DE
21 September 2022